Epistle

A Love Letter

INKBLOT BOOKS

Epistle
A Love Letter

All Rights Reserved
©2014 K.A. Thompson

No part of this book my be reproduced or transmitted in any form or by any means without permission in writing from the publisher.

Published by Inkblot Books
Vacaville, CA
www.inkblotbooks.com
ISBN 978-1-932461-34-3

Printed in the United States of America

Epistle

A Love Letter

MAX THOMPSON

Also by Max Thompson

The Psychokitty Speaks Out: Diary of a Mad Housecat

The Psychokitty Speaks Out: Something of Yours Will Meet a Toothy Death

The Rules: A Guide For People Owned by Cats

Bite Me: A Memoir (of sorts)

Visit Max online at his blog, The Psychokitty Speaks Out
http://psychokitty.blogspot.com

Books one of his people (K.A. Thompson) wrote:

Charybdis
As Simple As That
Finding Father Rabbit
The King and Queen of Perfect Normal
The Flipside of Here
It's Not About the Cookies
Rock the Pink

Visit K.A. Thompson online at her blog
http://kathompson.blogspot. com

For every kitty who was ever a newby kitty.

And for Buddah Pest
No, I don't know why
Just because.

**BEFORE YOU GET STARTED,
A WORD FROM BUDDAH PEST.**

OKAY, MORE THAN A WORD.

**HE REALLY NEEDS TO STOP TO
INHALE NOW AND THEN.**

A long time ago Max asked me to write a chapter for his next book so I did and then the editor lady was all "Oh, that's nice but it doesn't fit the format of the book and needs to be cut" and the Mom was like "Witch, I'll cut you, he worked hard on that" and Max was like, "Oh stop it, she's right, he'll have to write something else" and I was like, "I don't care as long as I get to write *something*," so I'm writing this and we'll save the chapter I wrote for something else, like maybe a guest post on Max's blog or something and I would tell you more but I wrote it like a year ago and don't remember what I said.

It took Max a long time to write this book and when I read it I said, "What? It took you that long to write a book this short?" but then the Mom told me that Max had written a lot more stuff and that the book was longer, like twice as long, but it was too close to other things he wrote before so she helped him edit it down so that it was really short, and then he wrote a lot more until it was almost long, and she went and cut more out so that it's short again!

Now, I was indignant (that means kind of annoyed) for Max because he worked hard but he says that's the breaks and that she was right, too, and that there's nothing wrong with a short book unless it costs as much as a really long book, but I don't buy books so that doesn't matter to me, I just want them to entertain me and since it's the Mom's money or maybe Max's money that buys books for me it can be short or long or a comic book or a blog post and I'm happy.

Max says that's the point of everything, so I'm right on track for my life.

Now, Max is an old guy and he can be a little grumpy and in fact he was grumpy before Grumpy Cat, who I really, really love because she's pretty and adorable and I like seeing pictures of her and I love video of her waddling away from the camera, but I have to live with Max and I'll never get to meet Grumpy Cat and that's a little sad, and Max is all, "Well, she's too young for you anyway" and I'm all "She's a grown up kitty, too" and then he told me that I'm an old guy, too, no matter how immature I am! I thought that was pretty mean of him but then I realized that I'm 10 years old and that's a senior kitty and I wanted to know how the hell that happened but Max said I'm supposed to make people think I'm the sweet one so I shouldn't say "hell." Still, Max is a lot older than I am, like almost 4 years older, so I can call him old and get away with it.

When Max wrote "Bite Me" I thought that was his last book because that's what old guys do, they write their memoir and then go watch TV for the rest of their lives, but he says there's too much stuff in his head that needs to come out and even though I think that's just hot air and all he really needs is a good long fart, I can't argue that people seem to like reading the things he writes and sometimes he even makes me laugh so I suppose it's a good thing he decided to write this even though I think sometimes he's ~~pawntif~~ ~~pontefacating~~ lecturing too much but that's what he does, he just says things and they're either right or they're wrong and he lets it be what it is.

Max doesn't like me and that's all right. I still listen to him because he sometimes has something to say I need to hear. He's my Hank, and if you know him, you understand what that means.

It means…everything.

Prolog

There was life before Buddah; I was still fairly young when the People brought him home with his nearly lethal cooties, but I remember the days before he became a constant pain in my backside. I'd lived a lot—in two different homes in California, then in Ohio, and then back to California—and in those places I saw a lot. I learned a lot, too, mostly from Hank the Dog and all the sticky little people who used to play outside my front window in Evil, Ohio. But still, I was young when Buddah showed up with his three-foot-long boogers and all that spastic energy.

He showed up just a few weeks before I turned four. Without warning, there he was, getting his funk and snot all over everything, including my people. And since those cooties were all over my people, they made their way to me, and you guys know the rest.

Buddah's mere existence in my world nearly killed me.

I think about that every now and then, the mortality attached to being alive. I talk about it enough that some of my friends online worry that I'm about to kick the bucket; given that I'm now 13 and a bit on the gravity-enhanced side I can hardly fault them for that, but as far as I know I'm just fine.

It's not just the end of life I think about, but the total of it, from the moments I can remember to the things yet to come before I do wander off to have an asterisk-kicking party with my friends at the Bridge.

I think about the kitten I was, and wonder… if I could talk to him, what would I tell him? What would I want him to know?

We're about to find out. I'm going to pop off on totally random things, I suspect, but just sit back and enjoy the ride through my head. And think of the very tiny, newby me, because this is my love letter to him.

Shuddup. You would totally write a love letter to yourself.

You're just jealous I thought of it first.

1

Dear Newby Max,

This is what I'm picturing right now: you're in the car of the Really Tall Guy and you're freaking out because he put you in a cage and then took you outside where it's bright and noisy and there are 2,741 things to be terrified about, and he took you away from the Crying Girl. You loved the Crying Girl; she played with you and told you every day what a good boy you are, and she made sure you always had food and water and head skritches, and this tall guy just picked you up and took you away without even asking what you wanted to do. All these things are whizzing by and you have no idea what they are, but you don't like any of it. It's scary, really scary. On the scary scale of 1 to 10, it rates an *Oh no I just peed myself.* There are sounds you don't know and smells that don't smell like anything you'd enjoy, and while you like this tall guy you don't really *know* him.

Dood, it's gonna be okay.

In about ten minutes the Really Tall Guy—whom you will soon decide is actually the Younger Human—is going to stop driving that blue box of doom, and he's going to pull your cage out of the car. When he does, the door to the house where you're going to live is going to open and this chubby lady wearing jeans that are a little too tight and a sweatshirt that's a little too big is going to practically fly down the steps while squealing *he's beautiful!*

That's you. You're beautiful. And you're about to rock that Woman's world.

Here's the thing, the Big Awful Hurdle you have to jump over before your legs are even strong enough to spring that high...she doesn't think she wants you. She thinks she hasn't gotten over Dusty, the Cat Who Came Before You, going off to the Bridge. In fact, she's pretty sure she never wants another cat, because Dusty was *that* special, and losing her hurt *that* much. But little man, she takes one look at you, and she's nearly hooked. Almost. She's standing on the other side of that hurdle looking over it and under it, but she's not knocking it over. She's not completely convinced, because inside the house there's a giant dog named Hank and she's truly worried what he's going to think and do about you. She's also worried he's going to scare you so much that you'll decide to live in a closet for the rest of your life…and you're going to consider it, because compared to you, Hank is a massive, hairy giant.

As big as he is and as foul as that breath he exhales is, don't worry about him; he's going to become your trusted companion. It'll take time and you won't ever get to where you're like best friends that share food and a bed (though it would be nice if you did that where I failed to), but he will win you over and you're going to spend a lot of hours looking out windows with him.

The key to your life is that Woman. She has a cat-shaped hole in her heart, and she's going to fight letting you in so that you can heal it. She will feed you and pet you and clean your litter box; she will tell you that you're a good boy and she'll play with you. But all the time she's doing that she's going to have an invisible hand blocking your way into her heart, and it's your job to get her to move it just long enough for you to make that leap.

Work on that leg strength; you're going to need to be able to make a monster jump.

You'll notice how she sits in that chair in front of the box with the bright light, and she moves her hands in front of it like she's a magician getting ready to show a really cool trick to an invisible audience, but then you hear all these clicking sounds. She's working at her computer. She's a writer, and one day she's going to help you get your thinks out of your head and into a computer, where you get to share them with the world. But first, you have to work a little bit, make her understand you're more than just the cat the Younger Human brought home.

You're a little guy, only 4 pounds, and there's nothing like a warm, soft kitten to start the melting process. When she's sitting at her desk, she tends to lean forward in the chair. Now, I know you want her lap because it's massive and squishy and full of warms, but try something different: jump up there and stretch out between her back and the chair like you're one long kitty sausage, and go to sleep. You'll be toasty and comfy, and she won't move because it's rude to wake up a sleeping kitten. Purr hard while you sleep; she can't resist that. She'll sit there for hours while she works, even when she's stiff and uncomfortable, because you're just a baby and babies need sleep.

She doesn't know it yet, but you're winning.

When she's sleeping, jump up on the bed. It's a pretty high jump because you're still so small, but you can do it. Jump up there and walk up her sleeping body, and then curl up on her chest or on the pillow right next to her head. When she opens her eyes, meow excitedly, like she's the best thing you've ever seen and you're so happy to see her.

She's not a morning person, like to the point I

kind of think she's allergic to morning, but catching her first thing works for you. She's still too sleepy to remember that she didn't want another kitty. All she knows when she opens her eyes and squints against the light is how wonderful it is to wake up to such furry happiness.

Purr. Purr hard. Get up and nuzzle her face and purr. Lick her nose, her chin, her eyelids. Get your face near her ear so she can hear your purrs and feel your whiskers tickling her neck. Tiny meows will make her hold you a little closer and make her sigh happily.

She doesn't know it yet, but that invisible hand she's had over her heart is slipping. Her fingers are parting, letting some light into those dark places where the hole is. And where there's light, there's warm, and she needs some warm in her heart.

As soon as her guard is down, you need to make her laugh. She can't keep everything so closed off when she's laughing hard. You don't need to do much to pull out all the cute because you're still a kitten and kittens are darned adorable, but you do need to work on the funny. Be impressively funny.

They key to that lies within the red dot. That dot is going to be your bane for the rest of your life, but for now, go after it with all your might. Chase it down like the mighty hunter you are. When it zips down the hall, run hard as you go after it. And when it zooms up the wall, jump like you've never jumped before. She's going to watch as you launch your sleek self more than halfway up that wall—push hard to get those legs to power you—and when you land with a disappointed thud because you couldn't catch it, she is going to laugh like that was the best thing ever.

And dood, it sort of is, because she's 12 kinds of impressed and amused, and she's letting go with the kind of laughter that only comes from finally dropping her guard.

Do it now, dood. Run for her, jump on her lap and meow while you give her a gentle head bump. Her heart is completely exposed right now, and you're going to leap right into it at right that moment.

You need to remember to do this, because this is the moment when you stop being the Younger Human's rescue and you start being Truly Awesome.

You're not going to replace Dusty, but she's going to understand that Dusty is still in that place in her heart, a giant furry soul, and there's plenty of room for you, too.

A lot is going to happen to you after that; you're going to have to move more times than a kitty should have to; you're going to come to an understanding with and have affection for that giant dog and in less than two years that's going to sting a bit; you're going to get a brother kitty named Buddah Pest and his coming to live with you is very nearly going to kill you.

That's going to be hard on everyone, especially you. You're going to hear the music of your friends' spirits coming all the way from the Bridge and be tempted to get closer so that you can hear it, but keep this in your head: it's not time. You still have a lot of things to do: books to write, wisdom to impart, and real live fresh dead things to eat.

When Buddah gets there, remember Hank. Remember how scary it was to move in with him. If you remember that and understand how scared he probably is, you'll be okay with Buddah. You don't ever have to like him, but if you can remember the way being afraid made you feel, you'll do good by him. It's always a good thing to try to understand how others feel; it keeps you from being a doosh. And no matter how much things bother you, that's not what you want to be. Not a doosh, and not the bag it comes in.

There's going to be some not so wonderful things in your life, but that's okay. The Woman is going to help you get to the wonderful things. She's going to help you start a blog so that you can tell the world about all the things that really annoy you, and while you're doing that you're going to meet some of the world's most awesome cats. You're going to make friends, and by doing that you're going to help the Woman make friends, some of the best friends she'll ever have. You're going to learn that just by being you and complaining online all the time that you can also do some good in the world. You're going to write a few books and earn some real money and spend it on saving boobies and buying toys for sticky people. You're going to come to understand a few things about living and dying, and you're going to be able to share that with the world.

But it all hinges on the Woman and being exactly the right kitty to fit into that battered place in her heart. If you can do that, you'll have everything a kitty could ever want, and then some.

2

Look, I'm not going to lie to you; there are some sucky things coming your way. Not too long after you turn a year old, you realize that you're about to embark on a journey you don't want to take, and you are going to freak the frak out. You're going to be stuck in a plastic box with bars all over it that gets jammed into the space behind the seat of a truck, and that giant dog Hank is going to drool all over you. It won't be pleasant.

Here's the thing…no one in that truck is exactly happy, except for Hank. He's just happy in general and where the People go, that's where he wants to be. If he's with them, his life is just fine. But no one wants to move; the People wanted to stay in that big house on the Air Force Base where you had premium window perches and fresh air to sniff, but the Air Force said, "No! You're too happy here! You must leave and go somewhere Evil!"

It sounds ominous, but dood, it's really not. It's a little scary because you're going someplace new, but you know what? This is going to set within you a kind of fearlessness about new places. Hell, you still won't want to go outside because outside is filled with vishus deer and squirrels and sticky people, and you'll always hate moving, but you're going to love exploring the new apartments and houses.

Remember that. Any time they tell you it's a new house, that means you're staying a while, so enjoy exploring all the little places you can hide and play. Discovering new stuff is about 13 kinds of fun, more fun than the People realize.

When you get to this place in Ohio, I want you to run around like your asterisk is on fire and meow at the top of your lungs. There won't be any furniture in the house, but the floors are slick tiles and the ceilings are high, so your voice is going to echo like no one's business. The Woman is going to tell you that you're Very Loud as if it's a bad thing, but you'll know better. Hank will know better and will egg you on. That's beautiful music, and it deserves to be heard all the way down the street.

And then look for the stairs. I know you're still not happy about living with Hank, so look for the stairs. He won't walk up them—he's afraid of stairs though no one ever really figures out why—so that gives you the entire second story of the house to yourself. Learn every nook and cranny upstairs, because it's your domain and you'll feel safe there. And once you feel safe there, you won't worry so much about Hank, and you'll be able to give him a chance.

And dood, seriously, give him a chance.

Sit on the stairs and look through the railings and talk to him. He's pretty wise for a dog, and he has things he can teach you. I listened, but I often think I didn't listen well enough or long enough. Hank has deep thinks that seep out between his words, and sometimes you have to do more than just hear him; you have to listen hard for all the things he doesn't say, and then take time to think about it.

Listen. Not just to Hank, but to everything around you.

Run around the house like your life depends on it; run for the sheer joy of hearing your paws slap on the tile and the wood of the stairs. Run because running is freedom. Run because you're going to turn into a fat cat, and maybe you can change that.

You have that awesome house with a ton of space to run, so do it.

And listen to Hank.

Everything is going to be fine.

3

Sticky people and Red Stupid Drinks.

Those two things are going to become a running theme of your life while you live in Ohio. Both will be sources of irritation and amusement, sometimes at the same time. Both are going to be reasons why you get fed late a few times and why your people act like complete dumbasses, but I have to tell you...as irritating as they can be, you might as well sit back and enjoy the show.

After you've been in the house for a week or two, the people are going to put perches up in all the good windows, the ones that look out the front of the house. The best one is in the office; that window runs almost all the way to the floor and you can see out of it when you're just sitting on the floor, but you get a perch anyway just to make it easier to relax and spend a lot of time there.

Oh, yeah...fair word of warning. Because it's low to the ground that means Hank can see out that window, too, and you're going to have to get used to that. He'll breathe on you and drool on you, and when you're 13 years old some hair is going to fall off your neck and I'm convinced that's why. All those days of rancid dog drool dripping on you and pooling under your collar, it makes sense that would be why you get a bald spot on your neck, right where it all ran under your collar.

You might want to ask him to back up a few inches. I mean, this is a dog who eats his own poop from time to time. I'm still grossed out thinking about how often he slimed me with his sticky saliva.

Yeah. Fecal-infested spitwads.

On one hand, you can't really blame him since he is a dog and all, but he's also smart and wise, and you'd think some of those brains would tell him that a poop picnic is 27 kinds of wrong, but no. If the people don't scoop the yard soon after he's been out there, you can bet that he'll scarf…and then barf.

That almost makes it worth it. Cleaning up a hairball is no major deal, but a giant splotch of wet, regurgitated dog poop? You will never see as much dry heaving as you will then. It starts with a grunt, then a gagging sound, and by the time the Woman gets those splatters of Gross cleaned up, she's trying to hork up her toenails.

Feel free to laugh.

If you spend a lot of time on that perch looking outside, you'll have a lot to laugh about. I wish I had looked outside just a little bit more, and I'm pretty sure I missed a few things while I was busy not looking out the window.

In any case, while you are looking out the window, trying to ignore the irritation of the fur-burning dog drool, your main entertainment is going to be the sticky people that seem to congregate in your yard. They all have yards of their own to play in, but for some reason they like playing right there outside your window, and they're loud.

Really loud.

Eardrum-piercing, nerve-shattering, teeth-grinding loud.

I won't lie to you; at first you're going to be afraid of them. Who wouldn't be? All that noise coming from something so small? The decibel level would be expected from something bigger than Hank, like a horse or a llama or a mother-in-law, but it's startling when it comes out of a creature so small and unformed that walking is often an issue. The fact that they're all so small and loud is frightening, especially when you realize that they can see you there at the window and decide they want to get to know you.

No worries.

They can't get through the glass or the screens, so they won't be pulling on your tail or your ears or your furs. A couple of times the Man is going to take you outside and let one of them touch you, but he won't let go and he won't let them hurt you. If you relax, you'll enjoy it. I didn't relax enough, but now I wish I had been more patient so that I could enjoy the pets more. Those sticky people were smarter than I gave them credit for and they understood when their parents told them to be soft and to be gentle; I was always afraid they wouldn't listen, but you know, not one of them every hurt me, not even on accident.

They're loud and all, but they're not going to hurt you.

The really little ones, the ones that walk like Frankenstein? They're going to call you "Math" and "Ki-ki" and even though you think it's humiliating, it's really not. They're trying very hard to say your name, so talk to them through the screen. Pay a little bit of attention to them, because it really does seem to make their day. When they giggle like that, the noise that is so abrupt that it almost makes you want to back up, it means you made them happy. If you meow back at them more often, they'll laugh a lot more, and that makes *everyone* happy.

If everyone is happy, extra food often follows.

I know that their little high-pitched voices kind of scare you, but they really do like you. And they are entertaining.

Even the People will enjoy them, and you're

going to spend a lot of time watching the People sit outside with the parents of the sticky people, and you're going to wonder why they want to be out there and not inside with you.

One word, dood.

Alcohol.

Stupid in beverage form, consumed from a red plastic cup.

When they sit outside, they consume Red Stupid Drinks and then they get all giggly and loud, and even though you want them to come back inside and be quiet, just chill and let them have some fun. Go hang with Hank. Trust me, you're going to wish you'd spent more time with him, and while the people are outside getting stupid, that's as good a time as any.

Hank is going to have important things to tell you and you need to listen. Remember what I said about listening for the things in between his words? Yeah, you really need to do that now. Hank's going to talk a lot about what he feels in his bones, and it's important. Now's the time to stop being a spasticat, to put as much of your inner kitten aside as you can, and start being a mancat.

Hank is going to need you to do that.

Man up a little.

A few months before you turn three, Hank is going to start feeling unwell but the People aren't going to know it for a while. You need to be there for him; don't be afraid to get close to him. Curl up on his bed for a bit and just let him feel you there. That's really what he wants, to just have you hang with him and to feel your warms touching him and your purrs vibrating through the bed. It won't cost you a thing to do that, and I wish I had been a little less afraid of his mass and more willing to get closer to him. I never did that, and it would have meant everything to him.

There's nothing wrong with getting close to a dog. He's a happy soul, just like you.

Pretty soon, he's going to let you know what's happening and he's going to want you to step up your game so that you can help the People when they realize that he's sick and he's not going to get any better. When winter is over and spring feels like it's settling in, they're going to finally understand.

By then you'll have a better idea about what's going on. Something is growing in his belly, and it's sapping his energy and is starting to hurt, and he knows that because of some medication he was on when he was much younger there won't be anything that can be done. The stabby guy can't operate and take the thing out the way they did with the Woman's head when she had something growing in it, because Hank can't survive anesthesia. The drug he was on ruined his liver, so he doesn't really have any options and doesn't want the people to know how bad it is until they don't have to worry about making a choice.

Hank won't want you to be really sad because he knows where he's going—and so will you—but he will want you to pay more attention to the People. No matter what, no matter how much they know letting him go is the right thing, they're going to be sad when he's gone. Little pieces of them are going to be broken, which Hank would never want. He'll be counting on you to suck it up and help them.

I won't lie, it's gonna sting a little when they take him out for his last car ride, but dood, it's okay. He loves car rides and this is one he wants to take. The day will be absolutely beautiful, with a ton of sun shine and just the kiss of a breeze that he'll feel reaching through his fur to tickle his skin; he knows where he's going and why, and it makes him happy that he gets to take that last ride with both the Man and the Woman. He feels so weak that walking hurts more than anything else ever has, but you know what? When they get to the stabby place and help him out of the back of the truck, he's going to stand up straight, hold his head high, and walk on his own power across the parking lot, to and across the sidewalk, and then inside.

The People are going to tell you about it later

but I want you to know now, so that you can be proud of him for them, and head butt them so they feel better. Dood, Hank walks so proudly into that good night; he gets inside on his own, but then he slips on the slick tile, and he can't get up. He can't ever get up. The stabby people bring him a stretcher and carry him into a room, but he never walks again.

And you know what? I know he was fine with that, because he had his beautiful day and a ride in the truck, and he walked in on his own terms. He wanted the People to see that he was all right with what was coming for him, and then when he slipped? Well, that let them know to not second-guess themselves about letting him go; it let them understand it was time.

Hank will always be a sweet and gentle soul, a very kind creature, so pay attention. He will teach you a lot about being a mancat, even though he was a big goofball of a dog.

You're going to miss him, even though you were afraid of him for a long time. You're going to do what he wants and comfort the Man and the Woman, but you're going to miss him in ways you never thought you could.

He was your friend before you realized it, and he always will be. For the next few years every time you look out a window and see a Golden Retriever you going to think, for just a few seconds, that he's back and you'll get excited…and then feel a little foolish. He was worth that kind of hope.

Never lose that.

4

The months before you turn three are going to seem like a lot of nothing; Hank is gone, and even though you accept it, you miss him. It's very quiet in the house without his giant paws clicking quickly across the tile, and you'll miss that sound, mostly because it was funny. He hated the tile and practically ran across it just to lessen the amount of contact he had with it. It's an unsettling quiet, but still…enjoy this time. This is the calm before the storm, so to speak. The summer you turn three will largely be spent sitting on the window perch in the Woman's office, sometimes while she works but often while she's outside, watching the sticky people almost every day, and listening to all their parents talk and laugh while they sit in the front yard.

Keep your eye out for something bizarre: the Man is going to put white Christmas lights in the tree out there, so that everyone has more light in the evening. But that's not the bizarre part. The bizarre part is that once those lights go up you're going to see a lot of bugs with tiny lamps in their butts show up. Dozens of them pop out of nowhere every time the people turn those lights on.

Dood…those bugs think that the lights are other lamp-assed bugs, and they want to do bouncy-bouncy things with them. And they try really hard, like it's all going to work out.

I know, right?

BUGS WITH LAMPS IN THEIR BUTTS!

Tons of things will be happening out there that are worthy of witnessing, so pay attention because if you miss it, you're going to hate yourself.

Quick, go take a look at the Man. Furry legs sticking out of his shorts, those giant feet with the hairs on his toes that stick straight up. Got a good look? Now, picture of bunch of doods just like him, that's the men of the court in Evil, Ohio. One evening, after I'd had my dinner and was thinking about going upstairs to take a nap, he went outside in his shorts and not much else, and the Woman followed. Now, it was too late for the sticky people to be outside playing, and it was a little cool anyway, so I had to go look out the window to see what was going on.

They'd put this long, yellow trash bag thing on the ground, one end at the top of a short hill, the other at the side of the neighbor's driveway, and started pouring water over it. And then, dood, holy frak, one by one those grown-assed men dove down the trash bag thing on their stomachs.

From the top of a hill to the bottom.

The bottom, which ended on a driveway.

You know what a driveway is made out of? It's made out of a lot of ouch, that's what. And you know why they did it?

To get the recipe for a special Red Stupid Drink.

That's it. Just to learn how to make a Stupid Drink. That was the only way the lady who had the recipe would give it to them, if they made a brave attempt at grinding all the skin off their chests and stomachs.

The Man ended up with a broken rib…and he said it was worth it.

Seriously, you want to see this. A bunch of pasty white doods sliding onto asphalt. For a *recipe*.

There will be parties and picnics and the smell of grilled real live fresh dead things drifting through the screen, and when it's time for your dinner one of the other people out there will make sure the Woman gets up and comes inside to feed you. You'll be sitting there thinking that you're going to starve to death, when all the sudden you'll hear someone call out, "It's time for Max's dinner!"

Seriously…if she doesn't get up right on time, they *make* her do it. And she's older than any of them, but that doesn't stop them from telling her what to do.

Enjoy every minute of it, because when the weather starts to cool there will come a day when the Woman puts you into the tiny, tiny downstairs bathroom with a bed, your litterbox, and some food and water, and you're going to get stuck there all freaking day long.

But that's not the worst part.

The worst is when you come out, all your stuff is gone. Seriously. ALL OF IT. While you're being tortured by having to stay in that little bathroom with hardly any air to breathe and the Woman is distracted by goings-on in the front yard, someone is going to sneak into the house and take *everything*.

She doesn't even notice! She sits outside in a chair under the tree with all the sticky people running around and their moms near her in their own chairs, and no one seems to realize that there are strange people in the house TAKING YOUR STUFF.

Oh, you can hear them through the closed door, their sneaky feet thumping across the floor and the grunts as they pick things up. You'll have that sinking feeling in your gut that things are most definitely not all right, and while you're choking on stale air and disappointment the Woman is NOT PAYING ATTENTION.

All you'll have left is your bed, your box, and

your blue plastic tomb.

Don't panic. You're going to get it all back, but I hate to tell you…in order to chase down the people that took it all, you're going to take another very long car ride. You won't have Hank drooling on you, but it will still be over three days in the car, and for a little while you're going to be sure that's what your life will be like from then on.

You'll even blog about it.

This is what my life is now, isn't it?

No worries; I mean, it sucks, but in a few days you're going to stop and get out of the car, the people will find you a new place to live, and they make the people who took all your things bring it all back.

Enjoy it while you can, because the litter box contents are about to hit the fan.

In a few months, the Younger Human is going to move in with you while he finishes school, and then not too long after that, the worst thing that will ever happen to you will happen.

Buddah Pest.

Look, no one even asks you if you want another kitty in the house. One day life is awesome, the next you can hear tiny little mewling noises coming from the Younger Human's bedroom. You're going to sit by the door and listen a lot, trying to figure it out, so let me warn you right now: do not, under any circumstances, play with your favorite nip toy near the door. You know the one, the little red candy bar toy. The one you play with the most. Because if you play with it near that door, there will come the moment when you drop it and then a skinny paw will shoot out from the under the door, snag your toy, and take it.

You will never see that toy again.

That's really only the start of how bad it's going to get. When you meet Buddah, you're going to be the better cat and will be nice and not all growly. Let's face it, he's just a baby, not much bigger than your whole head. He could be fun, and he's so young that he's probably easily trainable and you could turn him into your own dark little minion.

But...Buddah moved in with a lot of cooties that you just can't get away from, you get about 7 kinds of sick, and you come *really* close to going off to the Bridge. Your throat gets filled with snot-like goop, your head hurts, you're so tired that walking even a few feet is exhausting, and you lose your appetite.

Nothing is going to appeal to you. Not gooshy food, not real live fresh dead steak, not even real live fresh dead shrimp. The people will try to tempt you to eat with tuna water and even turkey baby food, but you just can't.

EPISTLE

Please, dood, eat. You won't want to, but you feel bad enough that you stop eating anything at all and it freaks the people out. Buddah won't care; he's half brain dead and doesn't have a clue what's going on. His entire existence is play, play, play and it's not his fault because he's only about 10 weeks old, but it's still his being there that did this to you.

They don't get rid of Buddah, though. Nope, he's there to stay. Don't turn your back on him, because when he's a kitten he thinks you're a pony and he tries to ride you up and down the hall, and when he's older he just gets all bitey.

I won't lie; it's going to be a hard year.

But you won't die. No matter how badly you feel, especially as you approach your 4th birthday, you're not going to die.

I promise.

5

Buddah. Always Buddah. It feels like everything is Buddah, all day, every day. He's a pain in the asterisk but you might as well resign yourself to him because he's not going away. There's also something a little off about him, so be wary. He can be calm and quiet one second, and a biting, claw-gripping, mean-spirited furball the next. No one will ever figure out what triggers him, so just be careful. Those spasticat moments aren't like a daily thing, sometimes not even weekly or monthly… just know that he's never going to be exactly normal.

Part of it might be because you got so sick when he came to live with you. He was just a kitten, maybe 10 weeks old, and he had already been in two shelters. His mother was a stray that wound up in a high-kill facility, and the Solano SPCA rescued him from that, and then the people adopted him from them, so he probably didn't get to spend any high quality time with his mother or littermates. And since you got sick so soon after he got there, you couldn't take the time to teach him how to be a cat. You were too weak to lay the smackdown on him when he got too wild and you were too tired to buck him off and pin him down for a lesson in feline manners when he tried to ride you like a pony. The end result is that he doesn't always understand boundaries or that he doesn't need to throw a temper tantrum to get what he wants.

He's going to be very much like a human sticky person for the rest of your life…one with sharp teeth and pointy claws. He'll never understand that it's not nice to bite someone just because they petted for 1.42 seconds longer than he wanted, and he will never grasp the notion of "soft teeth" as a warning to people. Or to you.

Oh, you're going to try. When you feel better, you're going to let him plop down right on top of you on the top of the cat tree. You're also going to let him curl up with you in a cat bed and lick his head because he's really bad about bathing for the first year or so. But eventually you're going to give up, because he just doesn't get it and you realize that Buddah is Buddah and will never be anything but Buddah. Something in his head is wired differently; maybe not wired wrong, but differently.

Don't feel bad about that, by the way. It's not your fault; it's not anyone's fault, not even Buddah's. The people see how he is and they're going to try a lot of different things, and they'll fix it so that you can live peacefully with him most of the time—mostly by getting him about a dozen climbing trees so he can be up high where he feels safest—but he's still a little bit Not Right, and there's nothing you can do about it.

Growling at him will work sometimes, but mostly, just avoid him.

Oh yeah, you're going to get really good at growling. You'll practically turn it into an art form, learning a bunch of different growls that mean everything from "back away, dood" to "I'm going to eat your face off."

Tip: don't try out a new growl on a person when they have food you want but they don't seem inclined to share. The only thing that does is irritate them, and you still won't get anything. Save those growls for Buddah. Chances are, he'll deserve each and every one.

The other sameness for the next few years...the M-word. A few months after you turn 4 the People are going to rent a house and move you out of the dark, dungeon-like apartment. And it's glorious, with stairs to run up and down and big spaces to play. Everyone is going to like living there, so of course something will hose it all up.

The guy who owns the house decides he wants to sell it just a year later, so you have to move again, and later you find out he loses it to foreclosure, which is both irritating (he had you in there paying the mortgage!) and amusing (hard lesson to learn there, eh? Don't try to sell a house when 90% of the inventory around is foreclosures and short sales going for 50% of market value.) [Note: I watch a lot of HGTV with the Woman. You're going to be bored by it, but you'll learn a few things. Like, when you can legitimately mock someone for bad realty decisions. Oh, and bad design. People have horrible taste. All people, not just yours.]

You luck out, though: the next house is even better. The people rent a huge place with beautiful wood floors and wood stairs, which makes for wonderful games of *Thundering Herd of Elephants* with Buddah, and rolling balls down the stairs at 3 a.m. is going to be 52 kinds of explosive, awesome fun. Buddah is going to be really happy here, because there are some super-high places he can get to and he loves being up high.

In fact, everyone loves this house so much and wants to stay there forever that it's no surprise when the owner of that one decides to try to sell it a year later. The people are going to get really mad about it because a few weeks before it went up for sale they asked if that was going to happen, and should they look for a new place to live? Owner-guy says it won't, so they relax and don't try to save a lot of money to move with, but then he does it anyway. Oh, yeah, the people are seriously upset, but the house right next door is for rent, so they get that one, move, and then watch as the house they love never sells and goes into foreclosure.

Now, the thought occurred to them to buy the house we all loved, but the guy had taken out so many loans against it that he needed to sell it for almost a million dollars and it was only worth about 30% of that, and while the people aren't the brightest bulbs in the pack they're also not stupid.

They're not only not going to buy it, they know what the end result will be.

Now, the lady that owns the house next door—which is just okay, not half as special as the last one—knows about the houses the people have rented before and how they have to keep moving through no fault of their own, so she offers them a 2 year lease.

You can see where this is headed.

Yeah. You're only going to get a little over a year in that place before she puts it up for sale, turns everything upside down with her Realtor wanting to show the house to strangers at odd times and getting really mad when the Man was asleep during the day so she couldn't…and then she loses it to foreclosure.

By now, the people are really irritated. They're tired of packing up and moving every year, and face it, they're not getting any younger. All that work is hard on old people. They don't want to do it again. It's not just the work of moving, either; it costs money every time they have to move.

So they finally do the logical thing. They buy you the house you're going to die in.

It doesn't have stairs, and it doesn't have high places, but it's yours.

You will never have to move again.

6

Dood, you're going to have a lot of jobs in your life. Sure, you're going to be this amazing writer that brings 2,694,178 kinds of joy into the lives of a bunch of people, but there are going to be things you *have* to do, and for them you'll get no accolades and no pay.

Seriously. You'll do a ton of work and receive no remuneration. It doesn't sound fair, but it's the price of being part of a family. You have to do your share.

Like, when a person gets sick. They're not feeling well; they're five kinds of sick and all they want is to curl up in bed and watch *The View Talks to Doctor Oz* and reruns of *How I Met Two and a Half Big Bangs* and not speak to anyone else or even blink more often than absolutely necessary, because they can hear the sound of their own eyes clicking inside their head and it's too frakking loud.

No one likes being sick; you won't like it when they're sick, either, because they turn into these nearly hairless, whining blobs of gooey flesh and getting them up to open a can of food for you is real work. Sometimes I think they forget we have needs, and when they're curled up in a giant ball of *Please Let Me Die*, we get hungry.

Your job is to be there when a person feels the way dog breath smells.

You might have to convince them that you're not trying to be annoying, that you're there to help.

[Note to people: we can purr at precisely the right decibels to heal some of your medical indignations and if we can't outright heal you, we can soothe the things that ache. You should thank us, not shove us off the bed.]

They won't make it easy. I found that out and hopefully knowing this early on, you won't need to work as hard.

Something I did not know when the Younger Human brought me home: the Woman has a lot of odd aches and pains, things on her that often hurt, but that the human stabby people can't do anything about. There are things she could probably do to help with some of the pain, like stop eating metric chit-tons of crap so often and drink water instead of fizzy things, but overall, she's an ouchy kind of person.

I was pretty much the typical crackhead kitten when I came home, so I didn't pay much attention to it, but after a while it was pretty clear: she needed my help. I was willing and I was able; after all, for the most part she was in control of the thumbs that open up cans for me, so I needed to protect that.

The problem? She didn't grasp that my intentions were honorable. I wasn't trying to plop down onto the parts of her that hurt the most because I was some sort of furry sadist; I was going to purr on her. Her hip hurt a lot, so as she slept I tried to drape myself over her for some vibrational therapy, but she always shoved me off. Her back always hurts, so I made sure that when she was bent over I jumped up on her to administer a little Max Medicine.

Did she appreciate it?

No.

I should have expected that, but I was young and was still feeling my way around people.

Just before I turned a year old, however, there was a lot of upset in the house because she had a new thing wrong with her, and it involved a lot of visits to the stabby guy, and tests that she failed (well, to be honest, I never once saw her study for them so I'm not sure what she really expected) so badly that the stabby guy sent her to a couple of other stabby people, and those doods wanted to cut her head open!

Surely I could fix that. If she would just lay still long enough, I could plaster myself across her face and purr hard enough fix whatever was in her head that had screwed up.

I tried a few times, and got nowhere.

"You can't fix this," Hank told me late one night. "There's a thing growing inside her head, on the underside of her brain."

"If I purr hard enough, it'll jiggle off and fall down her throat, and she can cough it up like a hairball."

Hank sighed patiently. "Not this time. You have to let the Man take charge with this. He'll make sure she gets fixed."

I wondered then if Hank's memory was shot. The Man had made sure that both of us had been fixed, too, and let me tell you, the stabby guy didn't do a damn thing to my head.

"Let her be," Hank said.

So I let her be. She still played with me and still she opened cans; she still made a lap for me and gave me head and chin skritches, so I was beginning to think Hank was wrong. If there was something wrong with her brain, how could she still do all that? She looked fine.

Six days after my first birthday the Man made her get up super early—it was still dark out, and she's allergic to morning so I thought that was kind of mean of him—and he took her outside. She took a pillow with her, which made sense if they were going to do things to her head; she probably wanted something soft under her head while they were fixing it.

I waited on the sofa all day, because when she came home I was going to double check to make sure she still had all the pieces and parts she was suppose to have, and purr on any that were ouchy.

I waited and waited, until dinner was several hours late and Hank was terribly uncomfortable because he needed to go outside to pee; at some point the Younger Human came home and let him out, but we were both still hungry. The Man came home when it was dark, fed us, and then let Hank out again…but he didn't bring her home with him.

Maybe they couldn't fix her?

"Patience," Hank said.

Patience was fine for him. He only needed to eat once a day anyway, and he only needed someone to let him out a few times. I needed to be fed a couple of times a day and the Woman was the one who did that most of the time. I needed my litter box cleaned. I needed regular tummy rubs. I needed her lap.

I decided he would bring her home the next day, and waited again. Hank waited, too, and waited so long that he did the unthinkable: he so badly needed to go out and there was no one home, so he had to go in the house, by the back door. He was so upset with himself I thought he was going to start crying, or maybe hide in the bathtub which would have been a big deal because the bathroom had tile floors and he hated tile.

I know he thought that lacked dignity, but I was pretty sure the people would understand and when the Woman saw how sorry he was she would pet him and tell him he was a good boy, and it was okay.

But again she didn't come home with the Man. He got home very late, and was so tired that he gave us food, cleaned up Hank's accident (and told him it was okay, he understood), and went to bed.

"Is she coming home?" I asked Hank.

For the first time, he wasn't sure. He curled up on his bed across the room from me, and sighed. "I don't know, Max. I really don't know."

He hoped everything was all right, but he couldn't promise.

On the third day, I think we both gave up hope. We napped the day away, jumping up when we heard the car in the carport; it was before dinner time, so that was a good sign, right?

But the Man came without her once again.

He fed us and let Hank out, ate his own dinner, and when he let Hank back in he plopped down on the couch and turned the TV on.

We sat next to each other in the living room and stared at him. We were both thinking the same thing: *tell us what's happening, and don't tell us she's gone forever, because we need her thumbs.*

"Tomorrow, guys," he said. "She's coming home tomorrow."

He didn't promise, either, but he seemed sure of it.

Man, I have never wished harder that I could laugh out loud than I did the day she came home, when she slowly shuffled back into the house. I wasn't trying to be mean, but come on; her face looked like she'd been punched by that Tyson boxing dood, and more than once. The end result was that she looked a lot like a Teletubby. The purple one. Tinky Winky.

She also had this thing on her face, like a little sling just above her lip, because her nose was peeing and she had to catch it.

Dood.

Her nose.

Was *peeing*.

For reals.

EPISTLE

She moved very slowly, and instead of stopping to see us in the living room and apologizing for being gone so long and turning our furry little lives upside down, the Man guided her down the hall into the bedroom, and she crawled into bed.

"She probably needs to sleep," Hank said when I got up, intending to go purr on top of her. "Something you should know: when she feels bad, she sleeps. Let her fall asleep, and then go to her."

I got what he was saying. When I was nootered, I wanted to sleep a lot when I came home. I purred myself better; since she couldn't purr, it made sense that I would go do it for her after she fell asleep. All I needed to do was wait, jump on the bed, and then lay across her face to purr as hard as I could.

I waited at least 20 minutes—I know it was that long because I counted: 1, 2, 3…all the way to 20—and then headed down the hall. She wasn't asleep, though; she was curled on her side and the TV was on, but when she saw me she patted the mattress and told me to come on up.

Now, I expected a sleeping person. I wasn't sure what I could do when she was awake. Past experience told me she wasn't going to hold still while I draped myself across her face.

"There's my Big Guy," she said when I was next to her on the bed. "I missed you."

She started rubbing my head and I plopped down next to her, and man, I don't know how it happened, but I started purring and I was the one who felt better.

It didn't take much longer before she fell asleep, but looking at how raw and battered her face was it didn't seem like a good idea to crawl up there and cover her head with my furry self, so I stayed there on the mattress for a while, until the Man came in and shooshed me away.

Fine, he didn't get it. She needed purr therapy, but I decided a few hours wouldn't matter.

She slept a lot for a couple of days, and on her third day home, the Man decided to take her outside for a walk.

I chit you not.

He took her outside for a walk, the same way he often did with Hank, but without a leash and I think he only avoided that because if he'd tried to put a collar on her she would have kicked him in the fun bits. She followed without complaining too much, and I watched from the kitchen window.

He guided her up and down the sidewalk in front of the house; I don't know if she didn't care that she was in her pajamas or not, but luckily no one else was out there to mock and make her feel bad about herself.

That will be *your* job, little man. No one else

gets to make fun of her, and if they do, you pin them down and then poop on something they love.

She only managed to stay upright and walking for about five minutes, but it was a start toward normalcy. She came back inside the house, went to bed, and ten minutes later I was up there on the pillow next to her head, purring as hard as I could without waking her up.

If only I'd been able to do it sooner; the next day she was awake a lot more than she was asleep, and she even ate real food while sitting at the table. I purred next to her head again that night, and dood, the very next day she put on real clothes and let the Man drive her someplace in the truck. If I'd been able to get to her right away, she'd have been fine in nothing flat.

Newby Max, you have to take charge. Listen to Hank, for sure, but when you know deep down that a person needs your purrs, don't let anything stop you.

For pretty much the rest of my life thus far, I've made sure I could get onto the Woman to purr her better and the evidence speaks for itself: she's still alive. Just a few months ago she was sitting in her chair when she suddenly had an odd pain hit her out of nowhere and she said it felt like her liver was trying to push its way out through an exit hole that didn't exist.

So I jumped onto her lap, pushed on her chest until she leaned the recliner back, and I draped myself across her stomach—all the while she's muttering things like "Dood, what the hell?"—and I purred. And purred. And in about 15 minutes she said the pain was all gone.

Coincidence?

I think not.

There was one really risky time when I couldn't purr on her—I blame the Man—and it took her a long time to get better.

It started with a tummy ache that turned into her feeling dizzy and lightheaded with tunnel vision, and then she started sweating really hard; cripes, she sweated so hard she had water pooling at her feet. And even though she was sweating, she was cold and shivering. It came on hard and fast and was actually a little scary, and she was in the bathroom trying to stop feeling so bad so I couldn't jump on her.

Well, the Man was right outside the (partly open) bathroom door and I didn't see him being much help to the situation, so I guarded the Woman.

Guarding means keeping away, so I did what I needed to keep him away.

Yep, I growled at him.

I ran inside to check on her—she still looked like the stuff crap is made out of—and then ran back out to growl at him some more, just to make sure he left her alone. I had to repeat it a few times, and he must have sensed I meant business because I didn't even get yelled at for warning him about what toothy things I would do to him if he bothered her while she was busy feeling like she was dying.

Still, I couldn't purr on her. She was either sitting there in the bathroom sweating puddles onto the floor or curled up in a tight ball of Ouch on the bed, which made it impossible to get to her tummy. And after about a few hours of that, when it stopped being just *Ow* and blood started being involved, the Man got all proactive and puffed out his chest and announced he was taking her to the Emergency Stabby Guy.

I couldn't argue with that. I hoped she wouldn't be gone for four days like she was when she had the thing taken out of her brain, but if I wasn't going to purr on her, she might as well see a professional. And the Man does stabby things for a living, so I trusted he knew that it was time for her to see someone with a giant butt bandage.

He brought her home very, very late and put her to bed, so I left her alone.

The next morning I went in to check on her and yep, she was still hurting, but she was lying on her side so I still couldn't get to her tummy, where it hurt the most.

Dood, she was like that for almost two weeks. She slept for most of it, and she slept on her side so I couldn't get to her tummy to help, and the Man kept chasing me away from her. When she finally did stay awake for a while and sat in her recliner, I was able to get onto her lap and gently pushed myself against her belly and purred really hard.

After a couple days of that? Well, she wasn't 100% but she was able to stay awake most of the day and watch TV.

It took a couple of MONTHS before she was 90% better.

If I had been able to get to her in the first few minutes, I'm pretty sure she would have avoided it all.

Here's the thing about people. They think we're being a royal pain in the asterisk when we crawl all over them while they feel bad. They whine and moan and push us away, because they just don't feel good.

Well, newsflash, we're not being a pain on purpose. We're trying to help. And if they would let us, they'd get better a lot faster.

Seriously.

EPISTLE

Cat purrs placed directly on what ails you speeds up recovery by 99.783%.

True story. I read it on the Internet, and the Internet doesn't lie.

7

THE TAO OF MAX

AN ASIDE TO PEOPLE ENJOYING MY THINKS, BECAUSE THEY ASK ME ABOUT THIS CHIT ALL THE TIME. I DON'T KNOW WHY, BUT WHAT THE HELL. I'M WRITING IT. DON'T TAKE IT PERSONALLY; IT'S JUST WHAT'S FLOATING IN MY BRAIN.

It's no secret; I'm getting older. By the time you read this, I'll be 13 years old. Maybe 14 if you're late to the game. I'll have been blogging for 11 years, and I'll have shared with the world how much sucky stuff can happen in a guy's life.

But the happy constant?

I'm getting older.

To paraphrase someone else, it's a privilege denied to a whole bunch of kitties and people. It's an unsettling fact of life that some don't get as many years here as others, and those of us left behind have these giant, open holes in our hearts where our friends or loved ones lived.

And it's not just that I feel bad that they're gone; I honestly think they're someplace awesome. I feel bad because of all the potential that went with them, and because I miss reading their blogs and laughing at the funny things and being upset at the sad things. The pain when someone else dies is pretty much a selfish thing; it's an okay thing, but face it, we're sad for ourselves.

I don't want anyone to really feel that for more than a couple of minutes when I'm gone. Maybe a day. I intend to live out my potential and when I go, it will be because it's time and I did all I needed to do.

That doesn't mean I'm *ready* to go; I'm not, but I've done pretty much everything a kitty can do, and I've had a really good life. When I go, I won't have any regrets.

When I was three years old and super sick, the Woman mused that if I got to 13, she would be really happy. That seemed like a decently long life for a cat; Dusty, the Cat Who Came Before Me, had a bad heart and lived to 13. Hank, my favorite dog ever, lived to 13. So I think 13 was planted in her head as a wish, because at the time she wasn't sure I'd even make it to four.

Now she's saying 13 isn't enough time. Her cat

Ataturk, the one who owned her when she was just a sticky person, lived to 15. So now 15 seems like a fine age to her.

I don't disagree.

But if 13 is it?

I'm cool with that.

I'm cool with 23, too.

What I don't want to happen, though, is for me to outlive my people. They're only in their 50s, which is not enough time for a person to do all the things they want to do (face it, they lose a good 25 years at the start while they're growing into non-sticky, thinking, productive people) and all the things they need to do. It takes their brains so much more time to cook past the point of being nothing but goo, and then they're chasing all the minutiae of Real Life, so they need those extra years on the back end. They need that time to move past the paper chase and onto the living phase.

Cats? We only need a few weeks before we jump paws-first into living, and then we're pretty efficient about it.

There's the thing…you people take too long to figure out what living really is. For the first third of your lives you're stuck doing what other people think is the right thing for you—and that's a good thing because when you're a sticky person you just don't have a brain that's been simmering long

EPISTLE

enough to figure it all out—and then you spend the next third of your lives just getting from day to day, working and paying bills and raising new sticky people, and from what I see online, a lot of you just aren't happy.

And why you aren't happy sounds like it's because you chose wrong when you were still lacking some fundamental pre-frontal lobe development. You went to schools that weren't the right fit because the grownups told you to go there, you studied things that you weren't passionate about because it seemed like a good idea for a career, jumped into the Ideal Adult Life which meant working harder than you wanted so you could buy a house and a couple of cars and assorted other Things.

Take a deep breath and a step back, boys and girls, because I'm going to impart some Max Wisdom.

Look at your cats. Look at your kids.

What's the one thing you want most for them?

It's not *stuff*, is it? You're not wishing that they get all the latest and greatest toys and bikes and a house made out of things they can climb on, right?

You're not wishing for them to get every single thing they think they want.

You're not wishing for them to grow up and work soul-sucking, backbreaking hours.

You know what you want for them. Deep down

you know.

More than anything else, you want them to be happy.

If they're happy, then they'll find the right path for themselves, one that will take them to whatever they want to be in life. Stabby person, legal shark, teacher of sticky things, dancer, actor, banker, counter-of-things, or even a person who sits at a computer all day and makes stuff up for other people to read.

You know why we cats bug the bejeebers out of you for gooshy food in the morning even if we have a perfectly good bowl of dry food already out and ready for consumption?

Gooshy food makes us happy.

You know why we purr on you, and taste-test your faces every now and then?

Because you make us happy.

That's the whole point of everything: to be happy.

Since we have the whole being happy thing down pat, it's all right that we get fewer years on this earth than do you. We spend 95% of our time here being exactly what everyone should be, and the other 5% is owed to visits to the stabby people, days when we don't feel well, and because you brought home another cat.

Watch us.

EPISTLE

We eat, we sleep, we play, we hunt—even if pretending, because pretend hunting is wicked fun—and we give you head bonks. We don't do that because we have to; we do it because those things are satisfying in and of themselves.

No one had to teach this to us. No one had to tell us.

We just popped into life knowing the purpose of life…to be happy. Other than needing your opposable thumbs, we were also born with everything we needed to be happy.

So were you.

But Max, you say, *no one can just decide to be happy. There are too many other things in the way: jobs and family and putting food on the table and all the horrible things that happen all over the world.*

Yes. Yes, you can. The details of existence and the decision to be happy are two different things.

It might not happen immediately, but barring medical things that fiddle around with your brain chemistry and get in your way, you can make the decision that you will be happy. No one else can do that for you. You can't rely on a job to do it, or other people, and you can't control everything that happens in the world, but you can make a fundamental decision for yourself: be happy.

It doesn't mean you have to change jobs; if you mostly like the one you have and it doesn't crush your soul, stick with it. Just figure out how to make it better for yourself. Maybe that means paying attention to the things you say and how you say them; people who complain and whine a lot—even when they don't realize that's what they're doing—make themselves feel as miserable as they're making the people around them. Listen to yourself; if you're a grump, do something about it. If it seems like everyone around you is just not nice and they don't seem to enjoy anything, take a hard look at the common denominator…and fix it.

I don't mean you need to become the Pollyanna Wonderdork of your place of employment. Just be a nice person. Treat the people around you with the same dignity and kindness you wish to be treated. Sooner or later you're going to realize that you feel happier, and people are treating you better.

If the job itself is destroying your soul, do something about it. What would you really like to be doing? Are you sitting in a cubicle every day, suffocating from the never-ending, mindless drivel that you have to do? Are you sticking with it because it's a paycheck, and you like to have a place to live and food to eat, and you have kids and pets and responsibilities?

Take a deep breath, stand up, and look around

you. It's not a prison; you get to leave. It's not the military (unless it is) so there's not much forcing you to stay there, other than the bills and feeding the kids and putting clothes on their backs. You can look for something else to make money; it's tough and makes you feel raw and exposed, but no one else can do what you can do for yourself.

What example are you setting for those kids? That misery is fine if it provides things? That taking someone else's crap is meaningful because it keeps the family in a big house?

You are your spawns' best example of how to live well and be happy.

Find your passion. Follow your passion. Teach them that growing up doesn't necessarily mean becoming a doctor or lawyer or TV anchor because they pay well. Those are jobs, not what they will become.

Teach them that growing up means finding out who you are, and honoring that. Teach them that there are many paths, not just one, and they get to run and play along all the paths that feel right, and that they can get off the paths that feel wrong.

It's never too late to explore a new path.

I would have to go back to school.

So? Go.

I'm 36 now; I'll be 40 by the time I finish.

Yeah? How old will you be in four years if you

don't go to school now?

I know what my passion is and what would make me happy, Max, but chasing it means downsizing and my kids won't have the best of everything or even most of the things they want.

No, but they'll have the best of you.

They'll see what matters most; if you're working your asterisk off to be the real you, the person that you really are deep down, they'll grasp something fundamental that a lot of people never do: it's fine to not have the big house, the best toys, or every little thing that they want.

And you know what? No kid was ever hurt by not getting everything they wanted, but a lot of kids have been cut off at the knees by getting it all.

You don't do your kids a favor when you give them everything.

You do your kids a favor when you allow them the gift of wanting. You give them a better gift of showing them that sometimes wanting something is even better than having something, and that by working hard to be real, to be genuine, and to be happy, is what feels best in the end.

A long time ago someone asked me if I was "a bit light in the loafers." They were half kidding, because I'm a freaking cat and I had turned down an invitation to be a girl kitty's date to an online function—and it wasn't the first time—so they poked fun at me for being a "confirmed bachelor" and hinted that perhaps I was ready to throw open the proverbial closet door.

(No, I don't care if there are no closets in Proverbs. You know what I mean.)

I have declined invitations for things online that could make others assume I'm in a relationship because…reasons. And *reasons* are good enough. I choose to love all of my friends equally, boy kitties and girl kitties, though I understand why some of them pair off and have mock weddings and dates and become A Couple.

It's fun for them. It makes them happy.

Their people become friends, often fast friends. Best friends.

Max, you can't help whom you fall in love with.

Yes. Yes, you can.

You perhaps can't control for whom your hormones start bubbling, and you can't help that you have a definite feeling of want, but you can sure as heck help whom it is you love.

Love is mostly choice.

How you act upon it is 100% choice.

My choice is to enjoy the affection I have for *all* of my friends. Yes, there are friends I sometimes think I have a teeny bit more affection for than others, but that's just nature at work. It doesn't mean I have to start treating any one of them better or worse; it means I recognize that I have more in common with a few, or someone in particular makes me laugh more.

I can feel the deepest affection for someone; that doesn't mean I have to act on it in a romantic way. That doesn't mean I have to label it as That One True Love.

I look at my people for that example. They love a lot of other people, but they *choose* each other. Every day, they make the choice that as long as the other one isn't being an abusive farkwad, they will love each other and be together. They can meet other people that are perfectly nice and who would be decent people to pair-bond with, but they don't allow themselves to make that leap; their chosen love is at home, and home is where they keep their hearts.

(Okay, take a moment to gag. I just did.)

Now, sometimes I don't get it because the Woman has a habit of saying perfectly innocent things in a way that makes me think she's mad when she's not, and I can see where the Man would think she's being all bitchy. She also looks pretty pissed off most of the time. But…she isn't. She just has a royal case of resting bitch-face and often sounds and looks annoyed.

EPISTLE

So he goes off to pass gas every night and she sits at the computer to make stuff up, and they make the choice to be mostly kind to one another and to love each other, and to keep their lives together as hassle free and nice as they can.

They things they do? Those things are part of their happiness. I know the Woman could go out and get a job that earns a better paycheck than she could by writing, but what would be the point? Writing isn't just what she does; a writer is what she *is*.

And the Man's job? The people had a lot of really lean years so he could go to school and learn to pass gas like a professional, but it was what was in his soul. He didn't just want to *be* a medical person; deep down he *was* a medical person. He helps people just about every day, and even the jobs he had before learning to pass gas were medical things where he could help people be more comfortable.

They didn't teach the Younger Human to chase the paycheck; they taught him to chase his passion, to find what he really is and not just something to do.

They taught him to reach for being happy.

And from what I can see, the end result is a good person who knows what he wants and is willing to work for it, because it's part of his personal happiness.

The choices of being alive are awesome.

Max…what if that paycheck IS what makes me happy?

Then go for it. The important thing is that you know it, and have chosen it.

Right now, I am going to go take a bath, eat some food, and go take a nap. Those things are pure happiness. And I'm choosing to do them.

8

Newby. Dood. One of the sucky things you're going to have to deal with by meeting all these great cats and people online is losing some of them. It's part of the balance of being alive; at some point it ends. It hurts, but it hurts because caring about all of them is a good thing. You'll notice that once in a while; you'll hear about someone you didn't know who has trotted off to the bridge and you'll think, "Oh, that's a shame, I feel really bad for their people," but when it's someone you know? "Aw, damn." And then maybe some tears.

Well, lots of tears sometimes. There are going to be some really cool cats along the way that you admire, and when they head off to the Bridge, you're going to leak.

A lot.

It's okay; it means they made an impact in the world, and that's a good thing. It means you cared, and no matter how grumpy people think you are, you're going to care pretty hard more times than you think is possible.

At some point you're going to wonder about the people, especially. Not *your* people, necessarily, but the people you connect with just about every day. You're going to surf blogs and lurk on Facebook and see a lot of anxiety and fear and sorrow, and you're going to have to watch them try to sort through all this *stuff* that seems like it's suffocating them, and there's not a lot you can do about it.

Well, you can listen, but that doesn't help them change things.

Dood, I've been listening to people for over 13 years now; most of them have their hearts in the right place, but they don't *think*. They spend so much time just trying to get from one day to the next that they don't stop, take a step back, and take a really hard look at the picture they're painting with their lives.

And it *is* a picture, dood. It's this giant, wonderful, blazing, full-of-every-color-in-the-universe, beautiful magnum opus, but they're so busy living in it that they can't see it for what it is. They exist in an incredible Monet-crafted masterpiece, but they don't step back far enough to be able to look past the brushstrokes and take in the amazing image.

Pay attention to them all. You're going to see some things common to a lot of people; I could never figure out a way to make them stop and look, but maybe you can. Maybe you can find a way to make them see that each brushstroke doesn't define the whole picture, and even the strokes that seem like mistakes don't detract from its breath-taking beauty.

You're going to be pretty much stuck living where the People live, and they will never consult you about the next M-word or even the next meal. It feels a bit insulting once in a while, but something I've come to realize: *they don't even consult themselves about those things.* They go where their jobs take them, they live in houses because that's what grownups do, they eat crap because crap is easy and life is hard.

They don't really *live*.

They spend so much time inside their own heads that they listen to the doubts that bounce around in there, and it keeps them from truly enjoying the experience of being alive. When they get knocked on their asterisks, it's just easier to sit there and wonder what happened instead of bouncing back up and delivering a hard sucker punch to whatever landed them there.

I mean, I get it; they have responsibilities and one major one is keeping the kitties fed and safe and warm. But they let those responsibilities tie them down, and when a person is tied down too hard they can't step back and really see.

Sometimes I think people believe they have to do these really big things in order to do more than survive, but really, it just means not squashing down all the things they really want to do because doing all the things they have to do seems more mature.

They all have dreams, but most people don't chase those dreams. Instead they spend huge chunks out of every day working jobs they don't really enjoy to pay for a house or apartment they only sort-of like and for things in it that seem like things people should have, and the real kicker is that they start doing it when they're pretty young.

I think that's one of the things the People eventually got right; when the Younger Human started college, he wanted to try a few different things, and they were okay with that. They didn't wag their pokey fingers at him and tell him he had to study something that would get him a great job; they wanted him to find out what all of his bits and pieces added up to. And he did, he discovered that what makes him happy is to get on a stage and pretend to be someone else with a bunch of other people doing the same thing, all to tell these big, wonderful stories that make the people watching them happy. It's like TV, but in person.

Yeah, he could have studied something that would get a job that would make a lot more money

EPISTLE

so that he could buy more things...but that wouldn't have made him *happy*.

And buying things...dood. People seem to think that buying things will make them happy, but really all it does is tether them to jobs and houses that they have to stick with to keep buying things that they think will make them happy...it's a craptastic cycle, and it doesn't work. Think about it: you have this basket and it's full of toys, and having all those toys should make you happy, right?

But then you go to play with something, and there's just so much *stuff* there. What do you do? Play with the red felt catnip thingy? The banana? The crinkle ball? Or one of the other three dozen things in there? You can't even see the bottom of the basket and can't really remember what's down there. There are so many toys that you can't really appreciate them all. You certainly can't play with them all. They're just going to sit there at the bottom of the basket, doing no good for anyone, and they'll make you feel overwhelmed.

A lot of people are like that; they keep getting all these *things* to make themselves happy when they can't possibly use them all. So all those things become Issues, and it stresses them out. They get something new and suddenly there's no place for it. What to do? Get a bigger place to live so you can have space for all your stuff? Getting a bigger place to live is just going to lead to getting even more stuff.

It makes them anxious.

The People have been there. They've had too much stuff, and what to do with all that stuff made them mentally itchy. Somewhere along the line they realized that all the stuff was not worth having an itch that can't be scratched; they dumped a lot of stuff by donating it to charity and now before they get something they usually ponder where it will live in the house. If there isn't a place, they don't get it.

Well, usually. People will always get things — it's something people do — but at least sometimes they think hard first.

You have to grasp this early on; I think I would have been a lot more satisfied if I had realized when I was still little like you that I really didn't need 20 catnip mousies and a dozen crinkly things. You can only play with one thing at a time, anyway. So when the time comes and you have some money of your own — and you will — don't spend too much of it on crap. You'll feel a whole lot better when you save it up and then use it for things like Christmas toys for sticky people and food and stuff for shelter animals. Seriously, dood. You'll get warm fuzzies from that, and nothing feels as good as warm fuzzies.

*

EPISTLE

The Woman has a Bucket List of things she wants to see; I think she knows that seeing those things won't necessarily make her happier than she already is, but it would be nice. She wants to see the Grand Canyon (yeah, I dunno; I think if she wants to see a big hole in the ground she could get a shovel and make one for herself, and when she was done looking at it she could turn it into a swimming pool) and she wants to go to New York to a museum so she can see Van Gogh's *Starry Night*, even though she has a perfectly good copy of it right here, hanging on the wall. She can even see it from her desk...but one of the things she really wants is to go see the real deal. She wants it to the point where it's almost a need.

Here's the thing from where I sit: why isn't she going to do those things? Sure, they'll still be there a week from now or a month from now or a year or two or ten from now, but that doesn't mean *she* will be.

Life can be unacceptably short; chit happens, and you think she would know that, what with having had the brain tumor and all.

It's a people thing. They keep putting things off, as if they'll have all the time in the world. They watch friends their own age die, and still they think they have time. They get sick themselves, sometimes really sick, and still they think they have more time.

You think they'd learn.

There's nothing like today. And if you want to get all goopy about it, there's a reason right now is called "the present."

It's a gift, dood.

Don't be like people.

Open that gift, and use the chit out of it.

9

No, I don't metaphorically float in my metaphorical loafers.

People and kitties are going to ask you this more than once, Max; you might as well face it now, so that you have time to accept that some of them don't see the bigger picture. Or at least they don't see the same colors in it that you do.

Well, that and there are some girl kitties out there who will want you for themselves in the worst way, and won't understand why you won't commit to just one of them.

"Why," the email asked me, "don't you have a girlfriend? Are you ...*you know*...?"

I get asked that roughly once a year. Why I don't have a kitty girlfriend, not about whatever ...*you know*... means. Whatever ...*you know*... means sounds ominous, but there's nothing ominous about me, so I guess I'm not ...*you know*.... And if I'm not, I guess I'm ...*don't know*...?

Whatever. I do not have a girlfriend and am not looking for one.

That doesn't mean I don't find many, many of the girl kitties in the blogosphere special and nice and wonderful and attractive. I do. Many are stunningly beautiful, some are quirkily beautiful, and all are wonderful...but so are the boy kitties. Some of the boy kitties are prettier than the girls, and I notice that.

But, even if I wanted a girlfriend, most of the special girl kitties have boyfriends, and I would never ever bat my beautiful green eyes at another boy kitty's special girl. That's disrespectful, and I like to reserve my disrespect for the People, not my friends.

Here's the other thing. It's the one good thing about the People having me nootered, robbing me of my fun parts. Since I'm useless to girl kitties when it comes to the things girl kitties need boy kitties for, it means my affections can be spread out a little. I don't have to like just girl kitties, I can really like my boy buds, too.

Truly, there's nothing wrong with a little mancrush, you know. I mean, I would not go so far as to say I carry notions of a bromance with any of my buds, especially since I've been nootered beyond all repair, but I'm free to seriously like all my kitty friends the same. If I find another boy kitty especially handsome, there's not a thing wrong with me saying so. If I find a girl kitty beautfulest, that's awesome, too.

Basically, I'm an equal opportunity crusher. I always thought Skeezix the cat was exceptionally beautiful, thoughtful, joyous, muscle-gifted, and had the *prettiest* eyes, and I loved him. I mean, I *really* loved him, and you will, too. That doesn't mean I had any bouncy-bouncy notions toward him. I think Diva Kitty is absolutely divine, with her shiny, velvety fur, and her grumpy I-hate-you glare, but I'm not pondering jumping her bones, either. I can have a little crush on any kitty, boy or girl, and it doesn't mean anything beyond that I find them fun and funny and I can't wait to read their blog every day.

So no. I don't have a girlfriend. I have lots of friends and I think they're all beautiful and I can crush on all of them no matter if they're boys or girls. And I doubt I'm ...*you know*... but perhaps I'm ...*polyfriendcrushish*...

You know?

10

All right, dood, here's something you need to know early on: your name is Max, but you're going to be called 1,537 different things. It depends on the Woman's mood, what you've most recently done, and how she feels about it.

Big Guy.
Mister Max.
Captain Crankypants.
Buddy.
Bubby.
Boobly.
Fuzzbutt.
Wonder Weenie.
Furry Little Bastard.

Look, it could be worse. She calls Buddah "Sweety" and "Smoochy Pie" a lot, but I think she's being intentionally ironic, because he's not sweet and definitely not smooch-worthy…even though I have seen her plant kisses on the top of his head.

It's not as if she doesn't recognize his

horribleness; just the other day I heard her say he was an evil little bastard because he nommed on the laces to her new shoes. He didn't get in trouble for it, she just called him that while she stared at the chewed up lace in her hand, and he wasn't even in the room when she did it.

The thing is, when you think she's going to hurl a name like *You Furry Little Bastard* to your face, she doesn't. Like this morning: she was still mostly asleep and I was curled up on top of her because that's just what I do in the morning, I suddenly barfed.

It was one of those surprise barfs; I tried to get off the bed, but I wound up leaving a bunch of my breakfast on her sheets right by her face, and then all over the brand new comforter.

Yeah, I expected her to be ticked off about it and was prepared to hear a name or two because that comforter was only like three days old and was not cheap, but no. Instead of getting mad she was all, "Oh no, are you okay?" and then carefully—managing to not get barf on herself—crawled out of bed. She freaking gave me a head skritch to make sure I was all right, and then stripped the sheets off the bed and started cleaning up.

I mean, I think I ruined that new comforter, but she didn't even act mad.

A while back, maybe two or three years ago, I

had to poop in the worst way. The problem was that Buddah got to the box first and fouled it so horribly I couldn't stand to get in it. I didn't even want to be in the same room with it, but there was no leaving that room, I had to go so badly.

I did the unthinkable. I pooped outside the box, and then went to hide, because I knew that was the wrong thing to do and surely she was going to be ticked off.

Instead…nothing. I heard her walk down the hall to the litter box room, then some cleaning up noise, and later when I finally came out of hiding she was all, "Oh, Mister Max, I'm sorry, I didn't mean to let the box get that bad. I'm sorry you had to go on the floor."

I know!

She apologized to me!

So don't try to completely figure people out or the situation you're in by the name they call you, because you won't. If she calls you Captain Crankypants, nothing bad is going to happen. Hell, you might even get a treat.

Yeah, I know. A treat. She rewards things like barfing and inappropriate pooping. I think it's a test to see if I'm really sick or not…if I eat it, I'm probably okay. If not, I might have cooties.

Remember that.

If you really want a crunchy treat, hock up a

hairball, then wait like 10 minutes and ask for a few crunchies. There's a 95% chance you'll get at least a couple of them.

You know what the worst thing you have to worry about when you start hearing the names-that-aren't-really-yours?

The pointy finger.

If she calls you Damned Furball, you haven't really done anything wrong. If she calls you a furry little son-of-a-beeyotch and has that pointy finger jabbing in your direction, she's really upset and it's because of something you did.

Buddah hasn't and will probably never figure the pointy finger out. He thinks it's a threat, and when faced with it he starts howling, like she poked him in the eye with it or she took away his favorite toy and *then* poked him in the eye. And if she gets too close with the pointy finger, he reaches out with his claws and slashes at her and sometimes he'll even try to chase her down to bite her.

We're talking full-on, run down the hall, chasing after her. She'll hide in the bathroom to get away.

Don't do this.

He doesn't get it; that pointy finger is just a finger, and it's never going to come near you. She will never (on purpose) jab you with it, poke you with it, or hit you with it, which kind of makes me wonder why she bothers, but all you need to know the first time you see it is that she's upset. Nothing bad will happen to you.

In fact, so much nothing will happen that I suggest you sit back, hike a leg up, and lick yourself.

She'll love that.

11

Dood, here's something you need to know, because over time it's going to change and you're going to be all, *What the Fructose?* because no one ever warns you it's going to change.

When you first come to live with the people, the house is going to be comfortably warm most of the time; I'm talking toasty warm, the kind where you feel sleepy and curl up on something soft, and then drift off into a very pleasant nap where you dream dreams about being fed real live fresh dead things that are cooked just so, and having a fountain running with cool, fresh water. You might even dream that you're curled up in the perfect sun puddle, and can even imagine the dust motes that float above your perfect, sleeping face.

Enjoy it.

It will not last.

The thing is, the Woman used to always be cold. As long as she could remember, she was cold from the inside out unless it happened to be a very hot day, in which case she was miserably hot and happily turned on the cold air blowing thingy during the day, and never once saw the irony in her state of being.

At night, though? If it had been a warm day it stayed warm in the house; if it cooled down, she turned the warm air blowing thingy on so that we were all happy and toasty…except for the Man, who was miserably warm but knew better than to complain, because she would tell him to go sit in a bathtub filled with ice and misery.

I think that might be half of why he decided to go pass gas at night instead of during the day; he could go where there were sane people who enjoy sane temperatures, and could leave the night time hots to the Woman and the cats.

Temperature-wise, it's a life of comfort, like a never-ending sun puddle but without having to be near a window. Somewhere along the line, though, a few years after the Woman gets that thingy that's not supposed to be there taken out of her brain, she stops feeling cold all the time and starts feeling warm.

All right, she starts feeling people-normal, which is a degree of warm that causes her to stop turning the warm air on as often as she did, which in turn means fewer curl-up-and-nap warms for you.

EPISTLE

The curious thing about this is that right about the time this happens to her—and she's happy about it, though I still can't fathom why—the Man starts feeling cold more often. There's nothing weird growing in his brain and the Woman thinks it's because he's getting older, but he's cold a lot.

You would think this means the warm air gets turned on more again, but no. Fans get turned on because the Woman can't stand being so warm, and the Man does not complain because he knows she would just tell him to put on more clothes, or go sit in a tub filled with hot water and misery.

There's no winning, dood. You're going to get about 11 years of sleepy warm niceness, then you'll be begging for winter to come every year so that she'll turn on the fireplace.

Don't try to understand it.

I've tried, and the only thing that's gotten me is brain cramps.

12

Stabby people.

You'll soon know who I'm talking about… those men and women who spend a gazillion years in school for the sole purpose of torturing dogs and cats and hamsters and the occasional horse or cow. Oh, they think they're doing something for the benefit of all petkind, but I've been there more than once. I see what they're doing.

They STAB us, and then say it's to prevent cooties. Well, I'll tell you what. If I had just STAYED AT HOME I wouldn't be out and about where cooties lurk and I wouldn't be exposed to the little floor-lickers responsible for most of those cooties.

They stick STICKS where sticks do not belong, and then declare it to be important because it tells them how hot we are inside. Well fark you, stabby guy, it only matters how hot I am OUTSIDE. If I feel a little warm on the outside, turn the freaking cold-air-blowing thingy on. If I feel too cold on the outside, tell the Woman to take me home and turn the fireplace thingy on. No one needs a stick up the asterisk to tell them if they're comfortable or not. And I can assure you, once that stick is there, no one is comfortable.

They ROB US OF OUR dignities, which mainly consists of flopping us over and removing our hoo-haws, and while I might never want to USE my hoo-haws, I should have a say in whether or not I get to keep them.

What bothers me most about the stabby people, though, is that they somehow make our people complicit in their actions. They convince our care-givers to take us there every single year whether we've demonstrated any need for medical intervention or not. It's been a year since we've seen Mister Max? Well, bring him on in SO WE CAN STAB HIM.

That's what the people get for their money—and they hand over real green papers for the stabby guy to get his freaky jollies—they get a stabbed kitty, an indignant kitty, and a really pissed off kitty.

You know what I do at the stabby place? What I do every single time?

I poop on someone. And I don't mean a gentle, easy-to-clean-up single poop. I EXPLODE. I let loose the bowels of war, calling forth the undigested bits and pieces from deep within my colon, the parts that still smell of bile and whatever awful things that release an odor so foul everyone in the building begins to gag. I will do this on the table, I will do this as I jump to the Woman's shoulder for safety, not caring that it covers her arm and chest and drips down the collar of her shirt into her boobie holder. I will do it as the stabby guy's assistant carries me to the back room to get cleaned off a bit; I will do it as they place me upon the scale that tells them how much mancat I happen to be.

I will empty myself in such a way that I'm frankly surprised I don't turn inside out, and so copiously that the stabby guy will inquire about the overall quality of the poop the Woman fishes out of the litter box every day, because surely it cannot be a good thing if I'm constantly passing foul, grayish, loose-but-not-liquid stools.

"No," she reassures them every time, "he just does that for you."

So you think they would bypass the annual visit and leave me alone, in the safety of my home, where I am not subject to cooties and strange people and yapping dogs in the waiting room. But no. They still want to see me, and I can only assume it's because I am awesome and they miss me.

When I was still very young and had only lived with the People for a few weeks, the Woman took me to the first stabby guy I would remember. I'd seen him once before, a day or two after the Younger Human brought me home, but he wanted me to come back in a few weeks because I was adorable and he loved me from the moment he saw me.

It was either that or because he didn't get a chance to stab me the first time he saw me and needed me to come back so he could do just that.

He was all right, as far as stabby people go. He stabbed me quickly and efficiently, and I was so busy listening to what they were talking about that I barely felt it.

"He's already doubled his weight since we got him," the Woman said. "At what point should we cut back on his food?"

I glared at her. *What the fructose, lady? I'm a baby. I'm hungry.*

Stabby guy lifted me from the table and stretched me out between his giant man-hands. "He's still very sleek and he's going to be a tall boy. Just keep food out and let him eat when he wants."

Eat.

When I want.

If not for the whole stabbing and shoving things where things don't belong, I think I would have liked him.

So when the Woman took me back to see him

again a couple of months later, I was fine with it. He liked me, he understood that I was growing into some pretty massive awesomeness, and he let me eat all the food I wanted. I didn't enjoy the car ride over, nor the sounds and smells of the dogs I could sense were there, but he was okay in my book.

Then he looked at my fun bits, and said I was old enough.

Old enough?

For what?

The Woman gave me a head skritch and said she would pick me up later.

Later?

WHAT THE HELL, WOMAN?

She left me there with the stabby guy and his minions, laboring to breathe under the stench of so many dogs that had passed through that room, and even though she said she would come back, I knew nothing good was going to come of this.

I never trusted that stabby guy again. He waited until I was asleep and did unspeakable things to me, and the Woman PAID HIM FOR IT.

I saw him again, a year later, and you can be damn sure he was the first to get the wonders of Max's Bowels.

I never saw him after that, though. I think it overpowered him.

EPISTLE

Oh, damn. I hope it didn't kill him. I never considered that before.

Eh...if I did, it was to the benefit of all those cats and dogs he was doing horrible, awful things to.

You're welcome.

13

There are 1,249,487 swirls of pale, ugly color in the tiles that surround the fireplace. I know this because I've spent many hours stretched out in front of it, either soaking up the warms or wishing for the warms, and when a guy is stretched out in front of the fireplace, it's a good time to engage in things that clear out the brain. Counting swirls, that clears the brain, and it's important to do that once in a while, to empty the gray matter of all its clutter, because when you do that your thinks get way better.

Not too many people seem to grasp this. They always have to be doing something: watching TV, reading, knitting, singing horribly off-key, playing around online…often doing more than one thing at a time. It's like everyone had to go and join the Cult of Multitasking, and left behind the calm of One Thing at a Time.

They're missing the joy of connecting with themselves. Instead of emptying their heads of the noise, they try to drown it out. That doesn't work; it only adds more junk on top of the pile of things that one would do better without.

Some people try; they sit on the floor with their hands on their knees, humming soothing words like *Ohmmm*, but even then they often have music playing. Music is nice, but it gets in there. It adds to the pile instead of taking away from it.

I like to just curl up on my bed by the fireplace, stare at it, and let the counting take me away from everything. Counting lets other things slip away, it's a focus that keeps me from adding to my pile of junk while letting the bits and pieces slide off and into nowhere.

And when I've counted high enough and have cut that pile down to nothing, naps happen.

Naps are always a good thing.

In fact, I think I'll go take one now.

A lot of horrible things have happened in the world since I was born. Just two and a half months after I popped into life, and right about the time I went to live with a friend of the Younger Human, 9/11 happened. I watched it on the giant box in the living room along with everyone else, though I didn't comprehend the enormity of it.

That was probably a good thing, what with being new to life and all. I didn't need to have my expectations squashed at such a delicate age. But I knew something wasn't right, because everyone was 13 kinds of upset, and I could sense that people were afraid.

Yep, you're going to be able to do that; it will be both an awesome thing and a worrisome thing, but you'll figure out how to make the best use of that particular super power.

I did what any kitty would do: I started running around the apartment like my asterisk was on fire until I was tired, and then I dropped right where I was for a long nap. I chased things only I could see, pinging off walls and furniture, until they were laughing about what I was doing instead of the awful things on the news.

Since then a lot of other awful things have happened; there's been more than one war, other people blowing other stuff up, people arguing and bickering over personal things, more things blowing up, more fighting… and not too long ago a couple of fantastical jerk faces (I'm being kind because you're young and don't need to hear the kind of words I really want to use) set off bombs in Boston during the big marathon.

If I paid attention (ok, more than I do. I pay attention but not *attention*) to all the stuff the talking heads on the news tell us everyday, I'd think that people are pretty awful overall, always trying to get things that aren't theirs, always hurting each other over some relatively unimportant personal point. Guns and bombs and knives and slings and arrows...people definitely do a lot of wrong things to each other in the name of *I Am Right and You Are Stupid*.

Even when it's not violent—cripes, take a look online. All the sniping and gossiping and doing things like Revenge Porn to each other...hiding behind the safety of a computer to reach out and virtually bitch-slap one another, inflicting wounds you don't have to see, emotional bleeding you don't have to clean up.

Yeah, it would be really easy for me to think that all people are despicable.

But they're not.

Really. They're not.

It's always the ugly zit that gets the most attention; the giant blackhead that puffs up and forms a pustule that you just have to squeeze. That's what get noticed, not the nearly flat little whitehead that no one but you really sees. That's the kind of thing people get upset over; they're getting their picture taken and that morning the biggest, ugliest zit *ever* pops up on their face, so hell yeah, they pay attention to that.

Some people are like zits. You hear about them because they've popped up and are making a nuisance of themselves, and they're so ugly that they command attention.

I don't mean ugly in a *what-you-look-like* way. I mean ugly in a *your-soul-is-broken* way.

All those people doing all those horrible things, that's what makes the news. That's what sticks with you when you're online, the mean and hurtful things you see. But really…people aren't so bad. They're not all zits on the buttocks of humanity. People are beautiful (don't tell them that, though) and routinely well-intentioned.

I know this because I pay attention. I look past the talking heads and go online to see what real people are talking about. I see what they're doing. A lot of them are doing a lot of good.

It doesn't take much more than a glance at the cat blogosphere to see the good in people. Every day they reach out to help each other. They're always pitching in to help each other with vet bills, people medical bills, transporting shelter cats to forever homes, moving households, personal care when someone is sick, and when someone dies.

That's the hard part, when someone dies. The CB is pretty big now, from maybe three or four cats when I started blogging to thousands now, and with numbers like that comes some sadness. You get to know a kitty, and then the person behind the kitty, and old age or illness catches up…even if you never met them face to face, it stings.

Sometimes they leave important things behind.

A while back one of the people passed away and left her three kitties behind. If not for the CB rallying around and donating money, time, and homes, those kitties would have wound up in a shelter, and that's not always a happy outcome. Instead of them winding up in that unfortunate situation, two people stepped up and offered forever homes for them; they needed help getting the cats to them, and it didn't take long before cars were lined up to drive for hours at a time to get those cats to the people who were promising to take care of them for the rest of their forevers.

I think what made the effort even more bittersweet was that the person who died had done that same thing only a bit over a year before, for another cat blogger who suddenly passed away. I think many in the CB remember Gentleman Beau and his mom, Mary. It was a gutting surprise when Mary died; Beau went to her sister's house for a while but the cats that already lived there just did not like him. He was heartbroken as it was; Beau was an older guy and between grief and being isolated because of those other cats, he needed a new home.

Rose stepped up; she had cats, too, but had patience and knew how to get them to learn to live with each other. She gave Beau a comfortable home and a nice life until he passed away a year later.

A big part of me regretted that I couldn't give Beau a home; he was an awesome guy but face it, I have Buddah Pest and that's about all I can handle, so I was grateful when he finally wound up with Rose. I was upset when he died, but I knew that in his last year he had a lot of love in his life, and I'm glad he wasn't there to lose another person.

And then in what seemed like a blink, Rose was gone, leaving her cats needing someone.

The CB is its own circle of life. When something goes wrong, the people who care for the cats step up. Hell, they've even *moved* in order to be there for another cat blogger in need of someone to help them with medical issues. They've formed such tight bonds that doing that didn't seem out of the ordinary.

It's not just the Cat Blogosphere, either. The places I surf around online to read—places like FARK and Reddit and Facebook—are ripe with stories of people reaching out to help someone else.

A few years ago there was a school bus attendant who got bullied mercilessly, to the point she was in tears, and the creepy medium-sized sticky people who did it were stupid enough to record it and put it online. One guy—I think on Reddit—started a fund with the idea that after going through all that, she needed a vacation. He only intended to raise enough so that she could go somewhere nice for a while to relax, but wallets across the world cracked open and the end result was enough money raised to allow her to retire. Like, over a million dollars. And the lady he raised the money for? She used some of it to start a foundation to educate against bullying.

I'm not sure I would be as thoughtful.

(Maybe I would be a little bit thoughtful. I would buy a lot of nip toys and real live fresh dead edible things, but I would at least think of doing something nice. Offer the SPCA a chunk o'change to take Buddah back, perhaps.)

Just take a look around whenever you hear all the dark crap the news spews forth. Most of the people around you are not even half as bad as the media would have you think.

Most people are basically good.

Well, other than the whole not giving us crunchy treats on demand. That's pretty mean, and they *all* seem to do it.

14

I have a bit of a wait problem. It hounds me day and night, nipping at my heels like a...well...a dog. A yappy little spastic wanna-be purse-sized dog. It's annoying as Hades, and burns almost as much.

It almost always starts like this:

"It's not time to eat, Max. You have over an hour."

I'm hungry now.

"No. Go find something else to do besides bother me."

So I go and find something else to do, until my stomach growls and I'm pretty sure over an hour has passed.

"Max. Stop it. I told you five minutes ago, it's not time to eat."

I'm hungry now.

She then sighs deeply, tells me I have *almost* an hour before food will be served, and then she tries to ignore me.

I don't think she got the memo: there is no

ignoring a cat whose food alarm has gone off.

Every five minutes, I remind her that I'm still there and still hungry. Once she's gotten to the "You still have fifteen minutes" drone, I amp it up and remind her every minute.

For some reason, this flusters her, and eventually she hisses through clenched teeth, "Dammit, Max, WAIT. Five more minutes. YOU HAVE TO WAIT."

I don't want to.
See?
That's my wait problem.

Every now and then—more often than I'd like, actually—the Woman picks me up and mutters something like "Hmm" or "Oof" and makes the Man drag out the scale to see how many pounds of awesome I am.

Most of the time, this is not a good thing; it is invariably followed by the d-word and my servings of gooshy food or crunchy treats become measurably smaller. It's happened so often that I'm frankly surprised that I get any food at all; as many times as that d-word gets tossed about, statistically I should owe them food instead of being given anything.

Luckily for me, the Woman sucks at numbers and frequently is heard to mutter, "Math is hard."

About a year ago, though, she made him weigh me and then declared that not only was I losing weight, but I was losing it too quickly. Apparently bad things can happy when a kitty sheds pounds too fast, and she wanted to slow it down.

Dood, this totally worked in my favor. They wanted me to be smaller and for my huge muscles to show through, but they didn't want my liver to explode, so she went with the only thing she could think of.

Max needs more gooshy food.

Now, Buddah and I always got a nighttime snack but it was just two or three crunchy treats, or as she called it, the *Shut-the-Frak-Up Snack*. At ten o'clock every night, I asked her—politely— for something to eat that wasn't dry crunchy food, and sometimes it took her a few minutes and 1,300 requests to get up and get us some snacky treats.

With the advent of losing weight too fast came the *OhMyGawd-Stop-Talking* serving of gooshy food. Instead of a couple of dry treats, we got to split a can of wonderful, meaty, tasty stinky goodness.

I wasn't sure how long this incredible thing would last, but I was still losing a tiny, tiny bit of weight every month, like an ounce or so, and apparently that was good enough for the Woman. For months she got up when I requested noms at 10 p.m. and opened a can for us.

I don't need much more than that to be happy.

I should have expected something to hose it up.

EPISTLE

You should always expect the good things to get hosed up.

The Younger Human—who no longer lives with us but instead lives with That Damned Dog Butters—had an important birthday in 2013, and the People wanted to celebrate it in a big way. So they decided to go to Las Vegas, where they were going to push him out of an airplane and then mock him for turning 30.

Or something like that.

While they were off doing birthday things without me, the Grandma came to stay with us. I like the Grandma, because she doesn't pester the bajeezus out of me and she's not stingy with the foods. In fact, when she's here, Buddah and I don't have to split a can. In the morning she gives each of us an entire can, and then does the same thing at dinnertime. In between (and after) she hands out crunchy treats like they're calorie-free kitty candy.

I don't go hungry when the Grandma is here.

She stayed four days, and right when I was starting to think I'd finally traded up, she left and the People came home. They were all three or four kinds of happy, and the Younger Human proved once again that he is a superior in the human species, because he survived being pushed out of the plane and even had pictures to prove it.

I admit, I was glad to see them. The Woman has a nice, squishy lap that I like to nap on, and it would have been a shame to lose that.

What I didn't realize is that the trade off was losing the extra gooshy food. The Grandma left, the people came home, and Buddah and I were back to sharing cans of food.

The number of treats dropped drastically, too.

The real horror, though?

The Woman thought I felt a bit heavier, and wanted to stop giving me food at 10 p.m. She held off for a bit, because it seemed kind of mean to have such an abrupt change, but dood, I could feel it coming, and I was not happy about it.

I'd almost forgotten about the threat to my food routine; the Man's birthday came and went, Mother's Day came and went, but then ON MY BIRTHDAY the Woman left to go drive a van for a boobie walk (this is one of the mean things about the Woman, Newby. She went to a boobie walk and then followed the walkers around in the van with the window open, and laughed and mocked them loudly.) That left me with no presents, no special noms, and the Man leaving the house every night right after dinner to go pass gas at the hospital.

That meant no 10 p.m. food.

I had no recourse, either; there was no one else home except Buddah, and he was as upset about it as I was.

"It's just for a few days," I told him. "She'll be home on Sunday. We'll get normal food times then."

But dood, she came home that Sunday night in time for dinner, but when 10 p.m. rolled around... nothing.

"You should be used to it by now," she said as she walked away when I requested a can for the 15th time.

She wanted me to eat dry food.

DRY FOOD.

Before she went to bed she doled out a couple of crunchy treats, but that was not good enough, and Newby, I was determined to win this.

It was on.

It was war.

Here's the thing the Woman tends to forget: I am a cat. I am, thusly, awake during a good part of the night, and I have discovered exactly where in this house my voice carries the most. I am not afraid to get up on the bed right next to a human head and shriek into an ear, and I am not afraid of then running to the most acoustically sound place and continuing the song of my people.

People value sleep as much as I value my food.

Bonus: the people don't hit, so I never have to worry about physical retribution. The worst they do is grumble and shake a pointy finger, and dood, that doesn't scare me one bit.

She headed for bed around midnight, and I waited. Three o'clock is a pretty good time to begin singing; she'll have been asleep for a couple of hours and will want nothing more than to keep sleeping. So I stood in the hallway, right outside the range of sight and the possibility of having a rolled up sock thrown at me, and sang as loudly as I could. Buddah looked at me like I was insane and was going to get us both into trouble, but I assured him that this was fair play and we would be fine. He didn't join me, but he didn't try to stop me, either.

I sang, and a few minutes later I heard her groan, "What the hell, Max?"

I kept it up, and a few minutes later she got up, looked around the door frame, and growled, "I am not feeding you."

I assured her that sooner or later, she would. Perhaps not this night, or even the next, but canned food would be forthcoming on my old schedule, whether she liked or realized it or not.

Satisfied for the moment, I let her go back to sleep. And then an hour later, I told Buddah that it was time for a rousing game of *Thundering Herd of Elephants*.

He can't resist that game. So we were off, running up and down the hallway, over and over, until Buddah did exactly what I knew Buddah would: he ran into the bedroom and leapt onto the bed, landing on the Woman with a soft thud.

She went *oof* and he ran off, leaving her to wonder what the hell just happened.

Twenty minutes later, I started to sing for her again.

She put a pillow over her head.

An hour after that, I jumped onto the bed and carefully crawled on top of her as if I intended to snuggle, and began bathing myself. Enthusiastically. With major contortions to make sure I got every spot I could.

She got up to use the facilities, and I followed, making sure she knew I was right there at her feet.

"Go. Somewhere. Else," she seethed.

So I did. As she crawled back into bed, I went back to the hallway, and sang my little heart out.

Lather, rinse, repeat...until the Man came home from passing gas and opened a can for us.

After that, I went to sleep, because there was a long night ahead of me, a night of singing and THoE and bathing on top of the Woman.

"I am going to turn you into guitar strings," the Woman moaned at 4:12 the next morning. "Or a tennis racquet."

Now, I've seen the Woman's guitars; they already have strings. And playing tennis would require some physical exertion on her part, so I was pretty sure I was safe on that front. So I kept right on singing in the hallway. It was a happy tune that I wrote especially for her.

I call it, "Feed Me Feed Me Never Let Me Starve." It's quite catchy.

It took a week; she held out a lot longer than I expected, and I was close to giving up. In fact, I was so close to giving up that I curled up in the chair next to hers in the living room one evening, and while she surfed online with her laptop, the TV on for noise, I whimpered.

I am totally not ashamed of it. I curled up and cried like a little girl, because in the end sometimes you have to do awful things to win.

She offered crunchy treats, but I stayed right where I was, meowing softly as if nothing in life was worth the continued effort.

And she caved.

With a heavy sigh, she set the laptop aside and got up. "Fine," she said, although she didn't sound half as annoyed as I expected. "You can have your canned food back. I'll just cut down on the dry."

Normally that might have upset me, but right then?

EPISTLE

I won.

Ten o'clock gooshy food returned, and I couldn't have been happier. So remember that: crying like a little girl totally works for you.

15

I frequently sit on the Woman's lap while she plays online; she reads a lot on the computer, like snarky news headlines at FARK, comics, blogs, and so many odd things on Reddit that there's no keeping track of them.

She also looks at an unhealthy number of pictures, and most of them are of other cats. I don't find this threatening in the least; she pets the kitties at home and rarely strays, so I can't really complain. One time she came home smelling of a strange kitty, but that was when she got to meet Diva Kitty, one of my long time blogging buddies. The only thing that miffed me about that was that *I* didn't get to go meet Diva Kitty.

Okay, I wasn't super miffed. Meeting DK would have meant going outside, and I am vehemently opposed to anything to do with going outside. There are evil, horrible things outside, like introoder kitties, vishus cat-eating deer, and the stabby place, so I prefer to remain inside where all my of my toys are and where the food lives (pay attention, Newby: VISHUS CAT-EATING DEER! I've never seen one but Skeezix did, and he had pictures of those deer and they look like they mean business.)

I at least got to know what DK smells like, since the Woman spent more than a couple of minutes petting her. I also got to smell what DK's bunny siblings, Fiona and Orlando, smelled like because she petted them, too. But I was mostly interested in DK, being that she's my bud and she's pretty grumpy, too.

She might even be grumpier than I am.

Once in a while I pay attention to what the Woman is looking at online, because every now and then she's looking at cat stuff, things like toys and food and climbing trees. And once, mother of Bast, she was looking at catios.

That caught my attention.

We have a patio. I can see it through the living room window. It's fairly useless as far as I can tell. The people never go out there to sit and consume Red Stupid Drinks the way they did when we lived in Evil, Ohio, and there are no sticky people playing out there for my amusement. Once in a while the Woman grumbles about the back yard being kind of trashy and not worth enjoying (because they're too lazy to make it look spiffy), but we have the freaking patio, and it wouldn't take a lot to turn it into Kitty Paradise.

So when she was looking at catios, I paid attention. I might have even touched my paw to the laptop screen, trying to get her to really see what she was looking at.

"Nice, isn't it?" she asked when I took my paw back.

I looked at her and then back at the catio on the screen. It was huge; there were see through walls and a couple of tall cat trees, and even a plush, comfy looking bed. Hell, yes, that was nice.

"Get a job, Big Guy," she snorted. "It costs about three thousand dollars."

Get a job?

Get a job?

I've written a bunch of books. I earn my own keep. Why the heck can't I have some of the money from those to buy that for myself?

I looked up at her again, wondering where all my income has gone. When I turned my head, though, I was face into her boobs, and then it hit me.

I donated all my money.

It went to fundraisers for boobies and shelter stuff.

Dammit.

I might really have to get a job.

EPISTLE

*

Here's the thing about boobs. Anyone can appreciate them. I don't care if you're a boy or a girl, nootered or not, grown up or a toddler, gay, straight, or what-not: everyone can appreciate boobies.

No, it's not that we all have some deeply seeded desire to sport spiffy racks of our own; in fact, having boobs wouldn't do me one bit of good. I'd probably step on them, and having stepped on the Woman's a few times, I'm pretty sure that's not exactly pleasant.

Having them attached to my person, though? That does me a lot of good.

Pay attention, Newby Max.

Boobs are useful. I discovered this when I was a tiny kitten, and I've found more uses for them as I've gotten older. At first, they were just these nice warm, wonderful things to curl upon as I napped. I was small enough then that I could—with a little support from the Woman's hand—fold myself into improbably small proportions and snooze upon her chesticles for hours at a time. They were comfortable and accommodating; forget the whole suckling thing, those boobs were the best bed.

As I got bigger—too quickly—they made for damn fine pillows. It didn't matter if she was stretched out on the bed or sitting in the recliner. I could almost always figure out a way to sleep on her stomach with my head resting on one. Sometimes I snuggled right up in between them and let the warmth just cover me like a soft little head blanket.

Okay, maybe not *little*, exactly. The Woman, being a sizeable human, doesn't have much that's little about her. But they've never been skull-crushing either. And that's not just to my relief; I'm pretty sure the Man wouldn't want them that big either, lest she roll over in her sleep and give him a black eye or broken rib.

We all know boobs are a thing of warmth and comfort. Babies know that right off the bat; they're grabbing for them before they can even focus. Teenage boys grab at them because they're teenaged boys and have bouncy-bouncy intentions. Women grab their own, just because they can.

I found more uses for them. Even though I still curl up on her, nowadays while she's in bed and grumbling things like "those aren't pillows" while I assure her that they most certainly are, I realized that I can do so much more with them.

In the evenings, starting at about 8:30, she and I watch TV together, until it's time for my pre-bed snack. She sets her laptop computer aside so that I have her entire lap and a good view of whatever's on the idiot box. Sometimes I pay attention—like when she's watching *Doctor Who*, because dood, it's DOCTOR WHO and you are going to freaking LOVE the Doctor—and sometimes I don't. A lot of people-TV isn't worth the effort, but once in a while she turns it onto something with a lot of people running and things going =boom= and I like those.

This is when I sit on her lap almost like a people, my butt against her thighs, my back against her stomach, and my head nestled just perfectly between her boobs.

Yeah, that's kind of like having pillows, but really I'm using them for neck support. This way I can drift off and I don't slide to one side or the other, bopping my head against the arm of the chair. She thinks I'm watching the TV, so she sits still, and I can snooze without her realizing it.

And then there are the times when I want to kind of hang out with my head resting on the back of the chair, and those boobs work wonders at keeping me from sliding down and onto her lap. I just need to get one back paw hooked onto her chest underthingy and the other planted right onto a boob, and I can hang out like that for a long time.

She doesn't mind if she's watching TV; she's not so happy about it if she's trying to "work" on the laptop (seriously…her "work" looks a lot like playing Bookworm and reading blogs and things at Reddit.) As long as I don't jam a claw into her flesh, she's cool with it.

And food! Holy heck, check her for food! A lot of the time when she sits there and has a snack, she get crumbs on her chest and doesn't even realize it. If it's something like a donut, it's totally worth the effort to wait patiently, and then when she's done, hop onto her lap and lick up the crumbs.

No, you're not doing anything freaky. You're just providing a service. A tasty, tasty service. On her boobs.

That's why I donate a lot of my book royalties to boobie things.

They're practical, helpful, and we need to save them.

You know, the Woman got into the whole Save the Boobies thing because of Jeter Harris, another cat blogger and buddy of mine. Pay attention to new cat blogs popping up, because you're going to really admire him. His mom had been walking in multi-day events for years, raising money to fight against breast cancer, and one year she was going to walk in San Francisco and invited the Woman to join her and some other friends.

She had to train for it, and that really hosed up my routine. I mean, I know in what order things are supposed to happen here: the Man comes home from passing gas and feeds us. Two hours later, I get the

EPISTLE

Woman up, escort her to the bathroom where I make sure she pees first, then takes her ~~drugs~~ medications, and then I lead her to the kitchen for her morning fizzy drink, because she's useless without that can of crap. Then I go back to bed for my nap.

She didn't warn me before things started happening out of order. She would get up before the Man got home and not feed me; instead, she grumbled a lot and put her shoes on and headed out to practice walking, then came home a giant, sweaty mess. It was tolerable at first, but as the summer wore on she was out the door super early and didn't get home until almost dinnertime.

Dood. When a person is outside all day long, they sweat a lot. And then they really do kind of stink.

I could tolerate that. She smelled funky but it wasn't horrible, and she did tend to shower fairly soon after getting home. The part I did not like was that she was not there to cater to my whims as they arose. The Man was home, but he was asleep. I spent all day alone—Buddah doesn't count—with my whims piling up like broken toys.

I'm all for saving boobs, but this was just mean.

I like routine; I like knowing what to expect. On days when the Man has worked the night before, I want the order of things to happen the way they always do. On the mornings when he has not worked the night before, it's not much different; Buddah gets him up at Food O'Clock, and then the rest of the morning follows as it should.

The months of Boob Walking training nearly did me in.

Oh, fine, I won't whine about it and neither will you. But it was a pain in the asterisk.

I think 2013 marked the 3rd year the Woman got involved in boobie events. If she'd just done one a year it would be like 4 years plus one failed attempt (she got sick just before a walk. Normally I'd muse that it was intentional to get out of the whole sweating thing but she was the kind of sick where the stabby guy shoves major pain drugs and anti-barf things at you and it takes lots of weeks to get over, so I'm thinking she wasn't faking.) That failed one was a two day walk she was supposed to do with Diva Kitty's Mom, but DKM wound up doing it all by herself.

I knew this year when the walk thingy was coming up, because the Woman likes to paint her hair hot pink for these things. It started out as kind of a joke, when one of her friends offered her a big donation if she would go pink and then go walk in Atlanta, but the joke turned out to be on him. After a couple of walks and about $15,000 in damage to his and his friends' wallets, she had to admit that the hot pink hair makes her happy. So now she paints her hair ahead of time, and that gives me time to mentally prepare myself.

Now, you'd think I wouldn't need to prepare at all, since it's not my furry asterisk out there walking, but her not being home impacts my life quite a bit. For one thing, I'm used to being the one who gets her up in the morning, and if she's not there I wander back into the bedroom for no good reason. But the important thing is that we have to rely on the Man to open cans for us, and he leaves the house to pass gas at night which means we miss our 10 p.m. snack.

Dood, that means I have to go ALL NIGHT LONG with only dry crunchy food to nibble upon.

That's just wrong. And that's why I'm warning you, because it is so, so wrong.

I thought the dyeing of hair only came with boobie things. You know, she signs up for a walk, her friends get stupid drunk and offer her money to turn her head all pink, she does it, and everyone's happy.

One day I walked out from the back of the house, having had a wonderful 3rd nap of the day, and there she was, with deep red hair.

We're not talking normal deep red hair, like

you'd expect on a perfectly normal of-Irish-descent type person. We're talking unnatural, crimson-like deep red. The kind of red you'd expect to find on walls. Or a car.

Not a head.

I suppose she wanted a reaction—I mean, she's an attention whore and that's the kind of thing attention whores do—but I just walked past her and headed for the sofa, where I could lounge and look out the window.

There are far more interesting things in our crappy back yard than anything to do with her hair.

Still...I knew it wasn't about boobs, because boobie things are pink. Plus, it was past Boob Walk Season and I was pretty sure there wasn't another one until after my birthday. So I paid attention. What the frak was the Woman up to, besides getting people to notice her abnormal style choices?

This is what I gathered:

There was a conference coming up, something to do with people who write crap and people who publish crap, and since she both writes and publishes crap, she was invited to attend said conference. Only, this conference was being held at The House of the Mouse, one of her favorite places in the world. So really, it was a "conference" and not a CONFERENCE; a bunch of crap writers wanted an excuse to go play at Disneyland.

EPISTLE

Her friend Murf, who has still not grasped that getting her to do odd things for donations isn't cringe-worthy because she likes them, offered her a big donation for another event she was going to, one that raises money for children's cancer. He wanted her to dye her hair purple at first—and she was down with that—but then decided she needed to go to Disneyland with the deep red wall-paint kind of hair.

Well...she really liked it. She went to Disneyland with her wall-paint-hair and enjoyed every minute of it.

So I kind of wondered what the whole point was, but then the kicker: to this event, she had to have her hair purple.

I knew she was going to like that, but...

But?

When she dyes her hair, she tends to also dye her scalp. And this children's cancer event?

SHE HAD TO GET HER HEAD SHAVED!

Dood, she was totally dreading having no hair and a purple scalp, but the rest of us were like YAY! because sometimes an embarrassed person is just 23 kinds of amusing, and 90% of the reason people give her money for these things is for the amusement factor.

I looked forward to the naked purple head for weeks. I was going to blog about it and post about it on Facebook, and mock her in ways that might make her cry.

The bummer? Her scalp was not stained by the time the event rolled around. It was a perfectly clean, although oddly lumpy head. I had nothing to mock. My fun was diminished by a factor of at least 23.

The upside? She *hated* not having hair, hated it in a visceral way, so of course Murf used head shaving as a way to poke at her before he would donate money to other events.

I like Murf. You will, too.

He has an evil streak.

It's not all about cancer. The Woman says everyone needs their "thing," the cause that means the most to them and something for which they will make an effort of contribution. She does things for cancer, and I like to do things for other kitties and—don't be surprised—sticky people.

My big thing every year is buying toys. You know how I said I wrote a bunch of books? Well, a big chunk of the money I made from those went to buy toys at Christmas for the sticky people whose parents needed a little help. I don't actually like to go outside to get the toys, but the People have unfettered access to my earnings and they go shopping for me.

This last year they took a couple pictures so I could see what I bought, and dood, I'm freaking generous! It took them two loads in the back of a Chevy HHR to deliver all the toys to the people who then give them to the kids, and after that they went out and bought another load of jackets, because there are a lot of kids going cold and I hate that idea. I have my fur and my fireplace so I'm always warm when being warm is a good idea; even though sticky people are sticky and belong outside and not in my house, I want them to be warm, too.

I don't know how much it all cost, just that most of my money went to it. And that's all right; I don't need a lot in the way of toys for myself, and Santa is pretty good at bringing me the ones I really like.

And dood, I'm not telling you this to pat myself on the back and be all, "Ooh look at me, I buy things for people." I'm telling you this because I think the Woman is right. We all need our thing, something that gives instead of takes. You're going to find giving is a lot of fun and it will be the second biggest reason that someday you're going to sit down and write this book for your newby self.

I can't go out there and walk for boobies and I'm damn well not shaving all my fur off or dyeing it, but I can give the People money with which toys can be purchased, and then I get warm fuzzies knowing there are some kids who had a decent Christmas.

(People…you should get warm fuzzies, too, because you're the one who bought my books.

YOU DID BUY ALL MY BOOKS, RIGHT?

Cripes, at least buy this one.)

16

Something to look forward to: you're going to be kind of a superhero. For reals. I mean, you won't get a cape or anything, but you're going to be the real deal. And it might be more important than anything else you'll do.

I've saved the Woman's life at least twice, and I did it long before things got to her that would have snuffed her out like a blobby pink cigarette butt. I pay attention to things around me, so when something's not right, I notice. If something is wrong and it serves to amuse me, I leave it alone. But if something is wrong and it will impact my ability to get crunchy treats, stinky goodness, or—you know—*living*, I step up and tell someone.

Knowing when to tell is important, dood. If a person is about to step in cat yak, you leave that alone. They probably won't get hurt, and it's really, really funny to see them hopping around on one foot while they whine about it. If a person is about to turn around and walk face first into a door, you leave that alone, too, because that's just some funny chit.

Once in a while, though, you have to let them know, because they have the thumbs. Look at your paws, dood. The Celestial Feline Design Committee must have been on break when cat paws came up for final inspection, and they forgot to give us thumbs. So we need to keep our people alive enough to use the thumbs they got when it's time for the opening of cans and bags of crunchy treats.

The first time I saved her life I was only a little over a year and a half old. The people had moved me to Evil, Ohio, so I was not terribly happy and considered not doing anything. Why should I? They made me move and I didn't have the Younger Human anymore, and it sucked big fat hairy donkey balls. But...I was old enough to have a little common sense, having just about outgrown the whole kitten crackhead phase.

Not that I didn't still enjoy some primo kitty crack—I still do—but I wasn't 90% stupid anymore. I was on the verge of becoming a real mancat, with sleek muscles and some real swagger. Even Hank noticed it; nearly every time I scored some people food with my cunning and stealthiness, he would say, "Oh yeah, you da man, Max."

Hank was pretty old by then and he knew stuff, so if he recognized my burgeoning awesomeness,

EPISTLE

then I was well on my way to becoming the quintessential mancat.

But…the superhero thing.

Something about the people: it's a bit odd, but they can't sleep unless they have air blowing on them, so there's always a fan running in the bedroom at night.

Another thing about them: they're not especially tidy. Stuff gets picked up from the floor every now and then, and once things on the bathroom and kitchen floors start to move on their own someone cleans up, but they don't tend to think of the unseen things that need to be addressed. Window tracks usually have gunk building up in them. Floorboards are coated with dust. Corners near the floor are almost always filled with whatever goop it is that likes to congregate in corners.

And fan blades? Those suckers spin all night long with no thought to the dirt and grime that builds up on them, and that dirt and grime eventually makes its way into the motor.

Since I'd had to listen to the fan every night from the time I was about 4 months old, I knew what it was supposed to sound like. I also knew what it was supposed to smell like—it was supposed to smell like nothing. So one very early morning, when the Woman was asleep and the Man was out passing gas, I realized the fan sounded funny, like someone was choking it.

It went *eee-eee-eee-eee* and then it farted. You know what a fan fart smells like? It smells like the Woman tried to cook up a mess of rubber bands.

I didn't know much about the anatomy of the fan, but I knew that fans aren't supposed to cry OR fart, so I jumped up on the bed and meowed in the Woman's ear.

"Cripes, Max, it's too damned early for food."

Yeah, lady, that's not what I want. I want you to wake up.

She tried to roll over, but I got in her way. Again, she moaned something about it being too early, and how she was going to turn me inside out by pulling my tail through my nose.

Clearly, reasoning with her was not going to work, so I did what I had to do.

I punched her right in the face.

Seriously dood, I curled up my mighty paw, pulled it back, and let it fly right into her face. I managed to get her nose, cheek and an eye, but most importantly, I got her attention.

Oh, she was upset at first, all "What the hell, Max?" but by then she was awake enough to smell past her own putrid breath and she sniffed out the awful fan-fart.

You have never seen a chubby woman get out of bed so fast. She was up and had the fan unplugged before I could even tell her why I woke her up. She stood there by the door, fan plug in her hand, and looked at me with wide eyes. "Holy hell, you little furball. You probably just saved our lives."

Yeah, well, it's what I do.

She dropped the plug and came back to bed, giving me head skritches as she sat down.

"A reward would be nice," I told her. "A few crunchy treats? Early breakfast?"

But do you think she saw fit to give me noms for my efforts on her behalf?

No.

She crawled back in bed and tried to cuddle me. CUDDLE ME.

It's a wonder I saved her life that second time. Sheesh.

The second time came years later, when I was 11 years old and we were living in the House Where I Will Die.

Hey, it's just a fact. Everyone gets all upset when I say that, but it is what it is, and what it is happens to be a good thing. The people bought this house for me so that I wouldn't have to go through the M-word again. I love the idea that this is where I will be for the rest of my life. Whether I have just one year left or ten, this is where I will die, and knowing that makes me happy.

One of the most awesome things about this house is the fireplace thingy. We've lived in other houses that had them, but those were the substandard sort that ate wood while they burned, and man… wood *poops* while being eaten by the fireplace thingy. I suppose under the same circumstances I would, too, but firewood poop is gray and gross and hard to clean up. The people hated cleaning it up, so they didn't let the fireplace eat very often. And to be honest, while the fireplace ate it also burped sparks, which I was not so fond of.

The fireplace in this house, though, doesn't eat wood. It doesn't burp or poop; it just has fire for me when it's cold out and the Woman turns it on. That's the cool part—it can be turned on. It has this little switch that she presses, and fire appears. Just like that!

Now, I can flip light switches, which is why the people don't put things I can sit or stand on near the switches because they have no sense of humor about me turning lights on in the middle of the night, but this switch is different and I haven't yet figured out how to flip it, so I have to wait for someone to do that for me.

When it's cold, she's pretty good about that. She'll turn it on in the morning for a while, and again in the evening when we're all in the living room and shivering. I even have a bed right in front of it, plus I have a nook right next to it, with a folded fuzzy blanket for me to nap on.

When the fireplace is on, I can curl up on the bed or even on the floor right in front of it. It blows out hot air at just the right angle so that it hits the floor, and I can stretch out there and bake on one side, flip over and bake on the other, then I move to the nook to cool down before doing it all over again.

I'm nice; I share the space with Buddah. He likes to get really close to it, right where the warms become the hots, and he stays there long enough that sometimes the people get worried that he's cooked himself to death. The people like the fireplace, too, though they stay across the room from it, because they are delicate and weak and they whine if they get too hot.

Still, she turns it on for me pretty much on demand in the winter, with the understanding that if I leave the room it gets turned off, or if she has to go to bed she turns it off.

That's fair, so I'm okay with that.

But one night I went to sleep in another room before she went to bed, and she was cold so she left it on while she watched TV. And apparently her brain farted, because when I went back out into the living room at 2:30 in the morning, the fireplace was still on.

Now, I know I could have plopped down to enjoy it, but I also know that an unattended fireplace is a bad idea. The Woman had it drummed into her from the time she was a sticky person that fire is not good at all, because the Grandpa had two houses burn down when he was little.

He was squirrely about fire and didn't let them use a fireplace at all while she was growing up, so the fact that she lets me have a working fireplace is a pretty big deal, and I know why she doesn't want the fireplace going unless there's someone with thumbs in the room to pay attention to it.

If I left it on, it might burp or something, and the whole house could burn down.

Granted, this is the house I want to die in but I don't want to take everyone with me, and I sure as heck am not ready to go right this minute. I haven't seen enough *Doctor Who* in my lifetime, and I kind of want to stick around for that.

I often sit in the hallway and sing in the middle of the night; I sometimes get up on the bed and meow in her face just to annoy her. So just doing those things wasn't going to work. I knew I might have to resort to punching her again, but without any fan farts to smell, she might think I was just being mean.

So I howled.

I stood in the hallway and howled hard, and

I howled long. I howled in the doorway; I jumped on the end of the bed and howled. I made sure it sounded like I was one twitch away from running off to the Bridge, and I kept it up until she sat up and asked what was wrong.

I howled in response and started walking down the hallway, and I didn't shut up until she followed me. When she walked into the living room I told her I loved the damn thing but I knew it wasn't supposed to be on, and what if it burped or something?

"Oh my God, Max. Thank you."

She knew what the Big Bad could be. She was really pissed off at herself for leaving it on, and was so happy that I had woken her up.

Did it get me any treats?

Do you really need me to answer that?

Maybe you'll have better luck.

There is something protective about the fireplace: it has a glass front, so most of its fiery burps and farts would surely be contained within it. That doesn't mean I trust it 100%. Who can possibly trust something that eats fire but never poops? The fireplaces in the old house used to eat wood and leave gray poop behind, but this one just noms on fire, and leaves a nice tidy pile of nothing behind.

I've looked through the glass when there was no fire going. There's a hole at the top, and I'm pretty sure that if it does let out a hearty burp, that's where any sparks would go. Straight up.

You know what's straight up?

The ceiling.

You know what I don't want to be responsible for?

Burning Ceiling Cat to smithereens.

So, yep, I keep an eye on it. The Woman hasn't left it on again, but she did it once so it's possible that she might.

Or the glass might fall off, and if that happens, I'm totally letting Buddah be the one to check it out. But no worries, if he catches on fire I'll grab him by the tail and swing him around until the flames die out.

I'm awesome like that.

This is all something to look forward to. You're going to be a *hero*, dood. A genuine, life-saving, non-cape-wearing hero.

17

Here's the thing, newby me: I could keep giving you a blow by blow account of your entire life and all the things you have to look forward to—the good and the bad—but then I would be robbing you of a lot of the fun.

It *is* going to be fun.

I mostly wanted you to know the important things: people are basically good and the ones you're headed for are going to really love you. Insanely love you. You have so many things to look forward to, like making a bazillion friends online, and writing books and even an advice column for a major online magazine called *Mousebreath*. The things that seem so big—like moving and sticky people and even Hank the Dog—will shrink down to their real size if you just take a deep breath and decide right off the bat things will be okay.

I know you're scared right now, because the world is whizzing by while you take the drive from the apartment of the Crying Girl to the House of the

People and it's a change no one ever asked you if you wanted to make. I'm here thirteen years later to tell you there's nothing to be afraid of. Not ever.

That's what I want you to know. Everything will be all right. Just be the best me you can be, dood, and your life is going to be *glorious*.

Swearsies.

ABOUT THE AUTHOR

I am Max Thompson. A cat. Seriously, a cat. If you don't know this by now, I'm kind of wondering why you bought this book...but you bought it, so that's what matters, right? You *did* buy it? Not pirate it? Because that whole file sharing thing loses me nip money every freaking year.

Heh.

No, really...I'm glad you're reading this, however you got your hot little paws on it. And when you're tempted to complain that there are misspelled words in it...I'M A CAT. Granted, an intelligent one not prone to the use of LOLspeak, but even those of us who choose to approach grammar and spelling with a modicum of correctness have our own ideas about how some of those words should be spelled.

Oh, and I'm still not looking for a good time or to have your babies, and you still get 4,382 Internet points for getting this far. You're awesome! Truly.

www.ingramcontent.com/pod-product-compliance
Lightning Source LLC
Chambersburg PA
CBHW061441040426
42450CB00007B/1153